Meditative Therapy

Publisher's Note

This publication is designed to provide accurate and authoritative information in regard to the subject matter covered. It is sold with the understanding that the publisher is not engaged in rendering psychological, medical, or other professional service.

Books in The Practical Therapist Series® *present authoritative answers to the question, "What-do-I-do-now-and-how-do-I-do-it?" in the practice of psychotherapy, bringing the wisdom and experience of expert mentors to the practicing therapist. A book, however, is no substitute for thorough professional training and adherence to ethical and legal standards. At minimum:*

- *The practitioner must be qualified to practice psychotherapy.*

- *Clients participate in psychotherapy only with informed consent.*

- *The practitioner must not "guarantee" a specific outcome.*

— Robert E. Alberti, Ph.D., Publisher

Other Titles in The Practical Therapist Series®

Creative Therapy with Children & Adolescents

Integrative Brief Therapy

Meditative Therapy

Metaphor in Psychotherapy

Rational Emotive Behavior Therapy

Meditative Therapy

Facilitating Inner-Directed Healing

Michael L. Emmons, Ph.D.
Janet Emmons, M.S.

The Practical Therapist Series®

Impact ✿ *Publishers*®, *Inc.*
ATASCADERO, CALIFORNIA 93423

ATTENTION ORGANIZATIONS AND CORPORATIONS:
This book is available at quantity discounts on bulk purchases for educational, business, or sales promotional use. For further information, please contact Impact Publishers, P.O. Box 6016, Atascadero, CA 93423-6016 (Phone: 1-800-246-7228).

Library of Congress Cataloging-in-Publication Data

Emmons, Michael L.
　　Meditative therapy : facilitating inner-directed healing / Michael
L. Emmons and Janet Emmons.
　　　　p.　　cm. -- (The practical therapist series)
　　Includes bibliographical references and index.
　　ISBN 1-886230-11-0 (alk. paper)
　　1. Meditation--Therapeutic use.　2. Client-centered psychotherapy.
I. Title.　II. Series.
RC489.M43E48　1999　　　　　　　　　　　　　99-7501
616.89'14--dc21　　　　　　　　　　　　　　　CIP

Impact Publishers and colophon are registered trademarks of Impact Publishers, Inc.

Cover design by Sharon Schnare, San Luis Obispo, California
Printed in the United States of America on acid-free paper
Published by **Impact ✍ Publishers,® Inc.**
POST OFFICE BOX 6016
ATASCADERO, CALIFORNIA 93423-6016

Dedication

To our Children, who represent the next generation of helping professionals: Brent and Scott Emmons & Heather and Jennifer Segal.

TABLE OF CONTENTS

Meditative Therapy

	Preface	xiii
1	Introduction to Meditative Therapy	1
2	The Process of Meditative Therapy	7
3	Paradigm and Perspective	21
4	Meditative Therapy, A Holistic Approach	29
5	Therapeutic Experiences in Meditative Therapy	37
6	Creative Experiences in Meditative Therapy	57
7	Helping Clients with Fears and Resistance	75
8	Meditative Therapy Outcomes	87
9	Facilitating Meditative Therapy: Procedures & Cautions	99
10	Enhancing Meditative Therapy	115
11	The Holistic Map	127
12	"Cleaning Cobwebs from My Mind" – The Case of Karrie	149
13	Roots of Meditative Therapy	161
14	Ten Important Points About Meditative Therapy	179

Appendices

A. Sample Fear Inventory Items	181
B. Willoughby Personality Schedule	183
C. Follow-up of Counseling Form	185
D. Meditative Therapy Follow-up Questionnaire	189
E. What Clients Want to Know About Meditative Therapy	193
F. Consent for Meditative Therapy Treatment	197
G. Creating Safety and Closure	199
References	203
Index	209

Acknowledgements

The authors and publisher are grateful to:

Chatto and Windus, Ltd. for permission to quote from *Letters to Aldous Huxley,* Grover Smith (editor).

The International Society for General Semantics for permission to quote from *ETC: A Review of General Semantics,* Weller Embler, Vol. XXXI, No. 3, September, 1974.

The Educational and Industrial Testing Service (EDITS) for permission to quote sample items from the "Fear Survey Schedule." Copyright 1969 by Educational and Testing Service. All rights reserved.

Joseph Wolpe for permission to quote from the *Practice of Behavior Therapy* (Second Edition).

Guilford Press for permission to quote from *Eye Movement Desensitization and Reprocessing,* Francine Shapiro, 1995.

Advances: The Journal of Mind-Body Health and Clair Cassidy and Lawrence LeShan, for permission to quote from pp. 5-31, 10: (1), copyright 1994, the Fetzer Institute and pp. 67-69, 13: (3), copyright 1997, the Fetzer Institute.

Appreciation

First and foremost, we appreciate the pioneers in psychology, meditation, and physics, who have influenced our conceptualization of Meditative Therapy. These include Carl Jung, Walter Frederking, A.L. Kitselman, Wolfgang Luthe, Daniel Goleman, Roberto Assagioli, Adlous Huxley, Jon Kabat-Zinn, Lawrence LeShan, Charles Tart, Francine Shapiro, David Bohm, Marilyn Ferguson, Karl Pribram, and Carl Rogers, who have met Rogers' challenge to "dare to investigate the possibility that there is a lawful reality which is not open to our five senses..." These predecessors give us the hope that Meditative Therapy will find a place in the repertoire of many practicing psychotherapists.

We wish to extend special thanks to our many clients who exhibited the willingness and courage to consult their Inner Source and to allow us to witness this process. In order to protect their privacy, we have changed any identifying material such as names, ages, professions, etc. Yet, we have remained true to their written transcripts and the essence of their therapeutic experience in order to reveal the workings of Meditative Therapy as accurately as possible.

Finally, a sincere thanks to Bob Alberti, who first demonstrated his faith in Michael's work in 1978 by publishing *The Inner Source: A Guide to Meditative Therapy*. His perception of both the value and the timely nature of MT inspired us to re-create *Meditative Therapy*.

*Perhaps in the coming generation of younger psychologists,
hopefully unencumbered by university prohibitions and
resistances, there may be a few who will dare to investigate
the possibility that there is a lawful reality which is not
open to our five senses; a reality in which present, past, and
future are intermingled, in which space is not a barrier and
time has disappeared; a reality which can be perceived and
known only when we are passively receptive, rather than
actively bent on knowing. It is one of the most exciting
challenges posed to psychology.*

— Carl Rogers

In our ongoing practice of psychotherapy with adults, couples,
groups, and university students, we have been presented with
a rich variety of therapeutic challenges. Our clients have
honored us with the opportunity to learn and grow as persons,
therapists and professionals interested in new methods and
research.

Holistically oriented, we use a variety of "inner" and "outer"
therapeutic modalities in our work. Our choice of outer methods
includes cognitive restructuring, person-centered talk therapy,
behavioral assignments, and couples therapy. Michael's valuation
of outer methods led him to pioneer in the development of
assertiveness training, and to co-author the seven editions of
Your Perfect Right, beginning in 1970. However, our work with
clients today would be incomplete without such inner methods as
dream work, active imagination, sand tray therapy, eye movement
desensitization and reprocessing (EMDR), and Meditative
Therapy.

Meditative Therapy dares to venture beyond the more widely
known methods and offer clients an opportunity to know
themselves in a "passively receptive" way. In our commitment to
a holistic, unifying, diagnostic, and healing approach, we reserve
time to check in with the client's "Inner Source" through
Meditative Therapy. We use the word "dare" because although
meditation and therapy are both familiar disciplines, the

integration of the two as a psychotherapeutic modality is relatively new and definitely exciting.

Although Michael developed and began using MT in the 70's (*The Inner Source: A Guide to Meditative Therapy* was published in 1978), MT's vast therapeutic potential remains relatively unknown. Perhaps this is because *The Inner Source* addressed both the general public *and* therapists, and was presented as a self-help tool, as well as a method of psychotherapy.

The confluence of three significant forces suggests a receptive climate for MT: Recent recognition and widespread use of other inner-healing processes, such as EMDR and Thought-Field Therapy. Increasing openness of psychotherapy professionals to new and non-traditional techniques as we enter the new millennium; and advances and refinements in Meditative Therapy itself. It is our hope that this book will stimulate more widespread MT applications and research among psychotherapists.

The Meditative Therapy process begins to lift the veil between the worlds of external and inner reality — for the client and the therapist. Becoming a meditative therapist allows one to witness and to facilitate the unfolding of the client's inner reality — a secret world of unending complexity —which can lead to increased healing and integration. We believe that Carl Rogers would agree that Meditative Therapy offers a window onto that "reality which can be perceived and known only when we are passively receptive" — an exciting new therapeutic challenge indeed.

Introduction to Meditative Therapy

Meditative Therapy (MT) represents a synthesis of two powerful healing disciplines: meditation and psychotherapy. The fusion of the ancient practice of mindfulness meditation with modern psychotherapy results in a natural, holistic therapeutic process:

> *Meditative Therapy is an inner-directed, therapeutic*
> *approach which facilitates a natural altered state of*
> *consciousness, allowing the client's Inner Source to engage*
> *in a holistic self-unifying and self-healing process.*

"The Inner Source" — the natural healing resource within every person — has been given many names throughout the ages, reflecting different disciplines and viewpoints. Spiritually oriented terms include the *higher self*, the *oversoul* and the *God-within*. Psychodynamic descriptors refer to the *superconscious* and the *collective unconscious*. Socio-biologists and other scientists use words like *biological wisdom* or *information processing system*. MT uses the term *Inner Source* to emphasize that a powerful flow of self-healing and self-actualizing wisdom exits within each individual. Whatever it is called and whether it is viewed as a spiritual or brain-directed process, the Inner Source can be accessed — and holistic healing facilitated — through Meditative Therapy.

During Meditative Therapy, the client closes his or her eyes and describes the inner events taking place, including thoughts, feelings, visual images and physical reactions. Within an atmosphere of patient non-interference, the client's Inner Source unfolds a wide variety of intricate, often beautiful, experiences to facilitate the person's growth toward wholeness.

The process is global and expansive, not narrow and specific. MT goes beyond situation-specific therapeutic approaches that focus on selected problems or targets. The Inner Source generates a holistic array of experiences dealing with the whole person — mind, body, and spirit — that specifically meet each individual client's needs and level of development.

For most therapists, the MT session will seem simultaneously familiar, new, and unusual. The Inner Source naturally integrates a variety of existing techniques into the treatment process. Some MT sessions employ flooding, desensitization, confrontation, awareness of behavioral patterns, and cognitive restructuring. As the process unfolds, clients frequently arrive at new insights. Other MT sessions may yield less familiar experiences. Abreactions may bring new intensity into the therapy room, as clients re-experience traumatic memories. Unusual occurrences — out-of-body experiences, light phenomena, spiritual insights, and odd physical sensations like tingling or whirling — may occur. Whether the MT session brings the known or the mysterious, the Inner Source experience remarkably fits each individual client's needs.

Meditative Therapy differs from most psychotherapies because it is an eyes-closed, inner-oriented process, led primarily from within by the client's own Inner Source. However, as in most psychotherapies, the therapist must create a context for client healing and growth. Although the therapist acts as a patient, non-directive guide during MT, an entire range of clinical skills comes into play both before and after MT. By using MT within a holistic, integrative approach, therapists can maximize the client's use of the MT experience. In fact, the Inner Source may point out the need for marital therapy, relaxation skills, or anger management. An optimum treatment plan should incorporate outer-oriented procedures as well as opportunities for the Inner Source to flow unencumbered for extended periods of time. In a holistic approach to client health, neither outer nor inner therapies should be used to the exclusion of the other.

Let's address some of the questions you may have regarding Meditative Therapy:

1. Do we really need another new therapy?
Let us answer this question with a brief story. Janet's grandmother was quite fond of her aging washing machine with the built-in wringer. After

a good deal of persuasion, she parted with it for an updated one with an automatic wringing cycle. After the first load, she commented, "It works better and I don't sweat so much." If grandmother were a therapist, she'd like Meditative Therapy.

2. Is Meditative Therapy really new?
Yes and no. MT shares the paradox Hermann Hesse's *Siddartha* uses to describe the river's secret: "It was always the same and yet every moment it was new" (Hesse, 1951). MT is a new way of looking at an ancient process. Mindfulness meditation accesses the meditative flow of inner experience, which we call the Inner Source. MT combines this process with the contemporary perspective of holographic brain processing; the essence is old, but the therapeutic formulation and application are new.

3. Exactly how does MT work?
No one knows for sure. The Inner Source therapeutic process is complex, yet deceptively simple. We make use of the holographic model to offer a working hypothesis for Meditative Therapy (see Chapter 3). This model accounts for the phenomena unique to MT, such as its ability to process individualistically, holistically, rapidly, therapeutically, and creatively. Yet, is the map the territory? Ask any traveler.

4. What is the holographic model?
Karl Pribram, a neuroscientist and brain researcher, states that information may be stored in the brain like a hologram. Holography records the wave field of light scattered by an object on a photographic plate in an apparently meaningless swirl. When a laser light strikes the plate, it can regenerate the original wave pattern, creating a three-dimensional image. Any piece of the hologram can construct the entire image. Pribram explains that the brain has a similar processing capacity, "wherein connections are formed by paths traversed by light, in addition to its more limited digital or linear computer-type connections" (Wilber, 1978). A specific memory may therefore be scattered throughout the entire brain, rather than limited to a precise location. The holographic processing ability of the brain also allows interaction with reality at a primary level, enabling spiritual experiences, rapid learning, and healing.

5. What client demands can MT meet?
MT is a bargain: It usually meets and often exceeds clients' expectations. The Inner Source addresses practical mental, physical, and spiritual

needs. MT can resolve the presenting problem, but it can also yield unexpected gifts. As one client put it: "This Christmas will probably be my happiest one, as has been this past six months. I credit most of this to Meditative Therapy, which has changed me, my attitudes toward life, myself, and others. I can truly say MT is one of the most wonderful things that has ever happened to me."

6. How do most clients react to MT?

Most clients react to MT in positive, life-changing ways. A group of thirty-six clients, who went through four or more MT sessions, responded to a follow-up questionnaire. Forty percent indicated that MT was the greatest thing that ever happened to them. Fifty percent said they gained greater understanding of the importance and meaning of human relationships, greater tolerance for others, and improvement in their behavior, as noted by others.

7. What is it like to facilitate MT?

Therapists report feeling a full range of responses during their clients' MT sessions, such as boredom, absorption, fascination, emotional intensity, and empathy. Janet describes her reaction as follows, "Most often I'm absorbed in tracking the workings of the Inner Source. I note the way a picture emerges from fragments of memories, thoughts, images, metaphors, and physical sensation. I watch connections occurring between current problems and past occurrences. While being present for the client, I see how each piece of the MT session fits into the gestalt of the whole client."

Michael states that, "Sometimes I feel the intensity of emotions as clients undergo extended discharging or abreactions. Once or twice, I've been afraid that an abreactive sequence might overwhelm the client or fail to resolve. I'm often awed by the unusual experiences that take place. I don't always understand why some experiences occur, especially ones that challenge my five senses. However, whatever the session entails, I usually come away with greater empathy and understanding of each person, as well as increased fascination and respect for the Inner Source process."

8. Has any research been conducted on MT's effectiveness?

At this point, research on Meditative Therapy has used a qualitative approach. Opened-ended questionnaires and interviews have all attempted to assess the effectiveness of MT based on client reports. Follow-up questionnaires included structured items, as well as open-ended questions to draw out clients' perceptions (Appendix D). We have also formulated a case study to include both client and therapist observations of the effectiveness of MT (Chapter 12). Additionally, throughout the book, case-study material illustrates the application of MT. The qualitative research to date points to the effectiveness of MT. Quantitative research will be conducted in the future to establish the efficacy of MT.

9. Do I need any special qualities or specific training to use MT?

If we were to design a training program for prospective MT therapists (beyond the preparation and qualifications required for your professional psychotherapy practice), course offerings would include yoga, white-water rafting, tightrope walking, chess, and travel to third-world countries. These classes would attempt to develop flexibility, courage, ability to trust, patience, and openness — all essential qualities for a MT therapist. Beyond these qualities, special training can prepare the therapist to deal with unusual experiences and intense abreactions that can occur during MT sessions. You can definitely learn the basics of Meditative Therapy from this book, but training workshops, supervised practice and experiencing your own MT sessions will increase your skills and confidence in working with MT.

10. Can MT fit with managed care?

As the saying goes, "he who pays the piper calls the tune." In most situations, managed care specifies a brief tune. Unlike many other depth approaches to psychotherapy, MT can meet the demand for short-term treatment. Although MT may open underlying problems, it also achieves resolution rapidly. Most clients can change positively in five to ten sessions. However, the therapist will need to check out the possibility of billing for extended sessions, as MT sometimes requires more than an hour.

11. How would MT fit with what I already know and do as a therapist?

Most therapists, regardless of orientation, would welcome a free consultation with a highly knowledgeable, skilled clinician. Meditative Therapy offers just this opportunity: MT consults the Inner Source, the "therapist" within. This consultation occurs within the overall therapy. All of your clinical skills come into play as you form the relationship, conduct the interview, arrive at a diagnosis, and formulate a treatment plan. MT can add depth and breadth to your existing therapeutic approach.

12. What populations would MT help?

Meditative Therapy is not like the delicate glass slipper meant only for Cinderella. Due to the versatile, holistic, integrative wide-ranging nature of the MT process, few client populations are contraindicated, except psychotic disorders or severe medical conditions which compromise the client's emotional or physical ability to handle strong abreactions. Of course, the therapist will still need to test the fit with clients; try out the method, observe client reactions, and obtain client feedback. Even if the shoe fits, some clients may not like the style. For the vast majority of clients, though, MT offers a means to a happier life.

Perhaps the best introduction to Meditative Therapy would be the direct experience of an MT session. The next chapter offers you the next best thing: a complete description of an MT session from beginning to end.

 Key Points

- Meditative Therapy is an inner-directed, therapeutic approach which facilitates a natural altered state of consciousness, allowing the client's Inner Source to engage in a holistic self-unifying and self-healing process.

- MT creates a synthesis between meditation and inner-oriented psychotherapy.

- The Inner Source process is holistic, dealing with mind, body, and spirit.

- The Inner Source uses integrative methods such as desensitization, flooding, confrontation, insight, and metaphor in pursuing therapeutic and creative goals.

- The holographic explanation of brain functioning provides a basis for understanding the Inner Source process.

- MT can meet managed care demands for time-limited therapy.

2

The Process of Meditative Therapy

That's the best feeling I can remember ever having, drunk or otherwise.

❖ ❖ ❖

I don't think I believe this! I feel now like it never happened, like it was just a dream for a second and went away. I'll never tell anyone 'cause they won't believe me. (laughs) *Wow! I just never thought of that at all. I thought about it to some extent, but never like that, it was so simple.* (smiles) *If I would have talked for thirty years I'd never have figured that out, I know it. This is the strangest thing that's ever happened to me.*

❖ ❖ ❖

What is the nature of an experience that prompts some participants to describe it in such excited terms? How does Meditative Therapy work, and why? Is the experience scary? Does it hurt? What are the results? Please join us for a "virtual reality" experience of Meditative Therapy and find out for yourself.

❖ Introducing Meditative Therapy to Clients

Allow yourself to pretend that you are one of our clients. Your previous sessions have established an open, trusting relationship, a thorough history, and a complete understanding of your presenting problem formulated in diagnostic terms. It is your third or fourth session and our discussion considers what types of approaches might be helpful for your problems. You have been told that among the variety of methods available, Meditative Therapy may be particularly valuable.

Our conversation begins

Therapist: "Meditative Therapy relies on the principle that we all have a natural self-healing mechanism within. I call it the Inner Source. Meditative Therapy helps you get in touch with your Inner Source."

lient: "Sounds interesting. How does it work?"

Therapist: "You either sit back or lie down, close your eyes, and allow yourself to be open to receiving help from your Inner Source. This intention seems to stimulate the Inner Source to respond."

lient: "Do I need to do anything else?"

Therapist: "Your job is to focus on whatever comes up, body sensations, images, feelings or thoughts, and to report it out loud. The idea is to watch passively, accept whatever you experience, and describe it to me."

lient: "What does that do?"

Therapist: "Concentrating on watching helps you move into an altered state of consciousness. The Inner Source flows most freely in this state and displays whatever you need to function and feel better."

lient: "Is it like hypnosis?"

Therapist: "In one way, yes. Like hypnosis, MT accesses an altered state of consciousness. It's also very different in that I won't direct the process: we'll leave that up to the Inner Source. My job is to support the process by being here with you and to record whatever you say. At the end of the session, I'll give you a copy of my transcript, so that you can read it out loud during the week.

I'd like you to read this handout on MT *(see appendix)*. It will give you a clearer idea of what MT is like and how it works. Next week we'll go over any of your questions and concerns. How does that sound?"

lient: "Okay. I'll read it over and think about it."

Next week, our conversation continues

Therapist: "Do you have any concerns or questions about MT?"

lient: "Well, I'm not quite sure if I can do it. Maybe nothing will happen."

Therapist: "There's really no way to fail at MT. Even the thought that 'I can't do this,' offers a place to begin. Remember that the Inner Source accesses a higher wisdom that knows more about what you need to see and experience than you or I do. I've learned to trust the process and just allow it to unfold. If you have trouble with this, I'll be here to support you.

lient: "What if I cry or get out of control?"

Therapist: "I'll be here to help you with whatever comes up. If you experience intense feelings, I'll ask you to just let it happen and at the same time keep watching. Observing your experiences and talking to me usually makes it feel less scary or threatening."

lient: "What if I get lost in it or can't come out?"

Therapist: "Even though the experience can be powerful or deep, you will remain aware of me and outer reality. You'll be able to talk to me and hear my responses. You can tell me about any fearful thoughts that come up during MT and we'll talk about them. Ultimately, you're in charge and the decision to continue or stop is yours."

lient: "So I can stop if I want to."

Therapist: "That's right. If you need to stop, just open your eyes. Then we can talk about what's bothering you. Hopefully, that will help you return to MT and allow the process to finish. It's usually preferable to stay with the process until a natural ending occurs. This allows whatever disturbance you might be experiencing to resolve on its own.

Beginning the Meditative Therapy session

Therapist: "Would you like to try MT today?"

lient: "Okay. What do I have to do? Do you want me to lie down?"

Therapist: "You can either sit back or lie down, whatever you're more comfortable with."

lient: "I'll lie down. Now what do I do?"

Therapist: "First, close your eyes and allow your awareness to shift inward. *(Pause.)* That's good. Now allow yourself to ask for help from your Inner Source.

(Pause.) Just allow whatever comes up to happen. Be a receptive observer. I want you to keep telling me what you're getting. If several minutes go by without your reporting, I'll remind you to keep describing what's going on. Also be aware of when a natural ending occurs. I'll watch the time, and if a natural ending doesn't happen, I'll help you find a good stopping place. *(Longer pause.)* So, what are you experiencing now?

❖   ❖   ❖

Since the Inner Source generates material to meet specific individual needs, I can't predict what you will experience. To give you some idea of the process, let's follow three clients through their first session of Meditation Therapy. Don't worry about keeping track of each client's journey. Just sit back and experience the process.

Beginning of the session. The session usually begins with a shift from conscious thinking to noticing inner experiences. Often the client comments on feeling awkward, fearful or resistant. With reassurance, the client usually begins to concentrate. You can see that the process is starting when the client shifts from surface thinking to deeper levels of experiencing. Inner Source content entails patterns, colors, visual images, bodily feelings, and thoughts.

First few minutes.

Eva: "So what am I supposed to be doing? *(surface thinking)* *("Just watch and describe whatever you see or feel.")* I see patterns of light, like I get when I first close my eyes. No color. Pinkish color now, with dark green lines on it. Just moving patterns and I'm getting a funny feeling on top of my scalp. I see a trike, a person walking down the street, a pair of hands." *(Inner Source)*

❖   ❖   ❖

Liz: "I feel a little tension about opening up my mouth and getting started. Kind of like being in a psychiatrist's office, the classical one, except you don't have one of those fancy couches. *(surface thinking) (laughs, takes a deep breath)* My heart seems to be pumping a little harder than what it was before. Some minor twitching underneath my left eye." *(Inner Source)*

❖   ❖   ❖

Ben: "I feel like I'm going to fight it because I don't trust my own sanity. I fear losing control to a certain extent. I'm thinking about the report I wrote today. Got it in on time. Have to remember to pick up milk at the store later. *(surface thinking)* (*"Try just focusing on bodily sensations for the next few minutes."*) Okay. Hmmm. Right now it just feels comfortable to lie on the couch. Feels like the blood is pulsing in my feet. Now my neck and shoulder area tends to be tense most of the time." *(Inner Source)*

❖   ❖   ❖

Five to ten minutes into the session. As the process continues, the Inner Source unfolds longer sequences and often accesses memories. A wide variety of mental, emotional, physical, and spiritual responses can occur: experiencing tastes, smells, dizziness, floating sensations, colors, patterns, trembling, twitching, singing, heaviness, warmth, anxiety, fear, depression, joy, thoughts, memories, etc. Each client's Inner Source employs a variety of unique combinations of holistic experiences designed to meet each individual's needs.

Eva: "That was weird, I could really feel myself hugging a big teddy bear. I had one when I was a kid."

❖   ❖   ❖

Liz: "Seeing Don sitting on the chair, when we were fighting. My mouth is salivating like before I throw up. I feel like I want to cry, but the tears aren't coming. Eyes feel jumpy. Picture of Dad and me as a baby. All the fathers I know...feeling sad." *(tears)*

❖   ❖   ❖

Ben: "I can't move my arms at all. They feel like chicken wings, but I can't move either. I'm surprised that I can do it. Just go to sleep and talk about it at the same time."

❖   ❖   ❖

❖ *Middle of the session*

During this stage, the Inner Source usually addresses two goals: healing and creativity. Keep in mind that the workings of the Inner Source vary according to each individual. However, generally the middle sequence of an MT session generates more lengthy and more intense material, uncovers the underlying sources of problems, reveals various emotional defenses, highlights strengths, or teaches new coping skills.

The healing goal is achieved through six types of responses:

1. *Discharging:* experiencing momentary visual images, bodily reactions, thoughts, and feelings.
2. *Extended Discharging:* experiencing longer sequences of visual images, bodily reactions, thought, and feelings, but without abreactive intensity.
3. *Reinforcement:* gaining a rewarding psychological, physical, or spiritual feeling.
4. *Understanding:* realizing the causes of one's difficulties, gaining insights, and arriving at solutions to problem areas.
5. *Abreaction:* reliving or re-experiencing various portions of disturbing or traumatic events.
6. *Treatment:* techniques from different modalities that alleviate symptoms such as desensitization, role playing, pointing out defenses, challenging beliefs, etc.

The creative goal is accomplished by the following three types of responses:

1. *Unusual Light Experiences:* seeing various forms of light such as colored light, light and dark interactions, or bright light.
2. *Parapsychological Experiences:* including precognition, past lives experiences, communication with discarnate entities, and out of body experiences.
3. *New Experiences:* unusual sensations outside of the normal parameter of everyday experiences, such as a spinning or

floating, changes in body size or shape, alterations in body temperature and time distortions .

As you watch the following sequences, I'll point out which of these responses that I see happening.

Three sequences from the session approximately ten minutes apart

Eva: "Right now I feel as if I don't have a family. I've always envied friends who have parents...so close. I've liked being around them, experiencing it, yet envious. The emptiness is in my stomach...numbness....*(discharging)* I have this one family picture. Everyone is alive, together. I've been noticing it this week. It looks like we were a normal family at home... Mom still alive. I still don't understand how I'm ever going to be whole. Jimmy eats donuts... We have to eat to feed that emptiness. *(treatment)* Maybe we're empty...fill that up...sleep, donuts, food. Part of my stomach is gone, a big gaping hole. In the picture, I'm next to my mother, so cute. It looks like I'm happy. There I'm whole. I'm three. *(understanding)*

"Floating along, but in a bubble — nothing can get to me. I don't reach out. Directionless, alone. Can't feel the flowers, look, but can't feel. Nobody can get close. Everybody is kept at a distance. *(treatment)* Spacy. Lonely. I love the earth, heavy jobs, heavy-duty yardwork. Love horses, earthiness of their bodies, but not real with it. Isolating myself...the bubble. If I would let myself feel, it would be panic. Maybe I would die. *(understanding)*

"Her death. That's what blew our world apart. I wonder if she knew what kind of lives we would live after she died. God. Linda McCartney died of cancer. A person can't help it. Everybody says Mom was such a good person. She had a lump on her breast, wouldn't go to the doctor. Maybe she knew, didn't want to go on — three kids, an alcoholic husband. Hopelessness. Maybe she gave up, I know that feeling." *(tears) (extended discharging)*

❖   ❖   ❖

Liz: "Going back and forth between Chad and his dad, my dad and me when I was a kid. How conflicted I felt because Dad was always so sad...depressed. I felt sad, but mad because he wasn't being a dad, wasn't there for me. *(sobs)* I'm mad because I've done so much work on this and it still keeps coming up. *(sobs)* I feel so sad for Chad not having a dad, so mad because he idolizes him. Seems like I can't do anything right and his dad can't do anything wrong. Hurts." *(extended discharging)* It doesn't feel like loving Chad, trying so hard, is enough. I don't want to feel like that the whole time I'm raising him, that it's not enough. I can see my mother on the bathroom floor. What a horrible mother she is. That was when we told her she was a great mom, when she was crying and depressed. I need to say that to myself. Tell myself what a great job I'm doing. I'm doing the best I can. My mom's favorite line, felt like such a cop-out. I wanted to say, your best wasn't even close to good enough. Maybe Chad will say that to me. I'm so afraid of messing him up. *(extended discharging)*

"On the floor. She tried to kill herself. I wanted to lay down next to her and cry because I was so scared. I'm talking to her, rubbing her hair, her face, telling her it's okay. *(abreaction, sobs)* *("That's good. Just try to stay with it.")* Take away the pills, get her settled in. I go into my room and cry into my pillow. *(sobs continue)* *("You can get through it.")* It's up to me to keep her alive. I'm scared, scared I can't do it. I'm tired, I want to stop now. *(sits up, opens eyes, stopping the abreaction prematurely)*

Therapist: "Let's check out how you're feeling. Then if you still want to stop, you can."

Liz: "Pretty raw."

Therapist: "I think it would be a good idea to stay with it, until you come to a better place, feel more comfortable. Can you give it a try?"

Liz: "Okay." (lies back down, closes eyes) "I hate her so much I want her to die and I'm so scared she will." *(curls up into a fetal position, sobs for five minutes) ("That's good. Just let it finish.") (abreaction)* "I want to give him everything like every parent does. Struggle. By giving him some things, he won't have others. Give him all the toys, he'll never know what it is to be poor. Can't experience all the possibilities in one life time. *(sighs; treatment)* I've been trying to cram it all into one." *(laughs; understanding)*

❖   ❖   ❖

Ben: "Looking at Denise. Watching, observing her. Our life is pretty chaotic. It's pulled me in. *(discharging)* I haven't always had a peaceful life, but usually more order. No routine. It's up and down, coming from her life and it affects me. *(understanding)*
"The idea of asking for what I need. I seldom think that way. The thought is going in...feels good, right-like. I'm asking her to take the phone calls so I can relax for a bit after work. *(treatment)* Feels good. *(deep breath)* Like I can breathe again. *(reinforcement)* Something she could do. She often says it's out of balance, because she's so sick. It's heavy for her, gives her a lot of guilt. *(understanding)*
"Strange. I saw a planet, red. Beautiful red light rays. *(unusual light experience)* More like a galaxy. I feel comfortable in my body. *(reinforcement)* I don't often feel that way. I can hear my voice for the first time. Interesting. It's like the body is an instrument rather than I am my body. Sensing the body, feeling it. Part of the chair, the floor, the air that surrounds me. I feel large, not small at all. *(new experience)* Voice sounds relaxed, bigger than normal *(deep breath)*. Feels like I'm leaving my body, very light inside, buoyant. *(parapsychological experience)* I'm so cognizant of my body, intrigued with how it feels. Don't remember the last time I really felt my lips. So calm now. A part of me is driving my body like a car. Whatever that is, that

is inside of me, is what I am. A lot of colors...deep purple, yellow." *(new experience)*

❖   ❖   ❖

❖ *Ending of the session*

Recall that prior to beginning MT, clients are reminded to be aware of a natural ending-point to the session. Sometimes these endings are quite obvious, with definite signals, such as a book closing, or the words, "the end." Often the client simply becomes aware of feeling calm and no new material comes up. At other times, especially if the session extends over sixty minutes, the therapist can watch for a good place to stop and suggest an ending to the client.

Eva: "Seeing her letter. She didn't sound sad to leave, maybe she did want to leave. It's like an open wound. A deep cavern, jagged edges, steep, impenetrable. It's closing up now. I know it's still there... but closed for now." *(opens eyes)*

❖   ❖   ❖

Liz: "Seeing myself as a teenager in the bedroom. I had satin bedcovers. I'm holding a pillow, leaning up against the bed. Hearing that album. Playing it softly. It's okay."
Therapist: "Does that feel like an okay place to stop now?"
Liz: "Yeah, I'm calmer. Let's stop now." *(opens eyes)*

❖   ❖   ❖

Ben: "I don't feel any tension. Jaws, back of neck so relaxed. I don't hurt anymore... nothing hurts. My body is so comfortable. I'm not getting anything else." (opens eyes)

❖   ❖   ❖

❖ *Responses after the session*

Debriefing the session allows clients to share their reactions to their MT experience. At the end of the session, give the client a copy of the MT transcript to read out loud several times during the week. Finally, remind the client to call if anything disturbing comes up during the week, if she or he feels unable to handle it.

Eva: "That was really interesting. I guess this eating problem goes back to Mother's death. It amazes me. The images, whole and hole, were really clear. I'm trying to eat my way to being whole. That's the first time I remember crying about her death. My aunt told me I laughed at her funeral. I can't remember that. I was only five. That always bothered me. It was good to cry. I feel more alive now."

Therapist: "There's more to your compulsive eating than you realized."

Eva: "It's pretty remarkable how I got that."

❖   ❖   ❖

Liz: "That was really intense. I didn't expect it because I thought I had dealt with those feelings. This went much deeper than any therapy I've ever done. It went to the bottom. I didn't realize how deep it was until I came out. I'm glad you helped me go on."

Therapist: "You were really brave to stay with it. I could feel how hard that was for you. If you get any more intense reactions or if you start feeling "raw" again, give me a call."

Liz: "Thanks. I think I'll be fine, but I'll call if I need to."

Therapist: "Good. No toughing it out."

Liz: "Me?" *(laughs)*

Therapist: "How are you doing now?"

Liz: "Pretty exhausted."

Therapist: "Why don't you have a sip of water and walk around a little before leaving. Make sure you feel ready to drive."

Liz: "That's probably a good idea."

❖   ❖   ❖

Ben: "Weird and wild. I felt like I was in a space suit. I got in touch with a spiritual resource that's inside of me. I need to remember I have that...now more than ever with Denise so ill."

Therapist: "It's really been hard on you to handle so much lately."

Ben: "Yeah. Just when I think I can't take it, I get a little break and then it's okay. I feel more energy now."

Therapist: "How could you stay in touch with that this week?"

Ben: "I used to meditate. Maybe I could start that again."

Therapist: "That sounds good."

Ben: "I'll try it. Maybe that's something else Denise could do, just let me have that time to myself to meditate."

Therapist: "Here's a copy of your MT session. I'd like you to read it over several times out loud this week. Then next week we can talk about it."

Ben: "Okay, see you next week."

❖   ❖   ❖

Debriefing gives the therapist a chance to make sure the client has returned to a normal state of consciousness. By talking, having a drink of water, or just getting up and moving around, clients become reoriented and can safely leave the office.

Our conversation continues

Therapist: "Well, how was your first MT experience?"

lient: "That session seemed like it lasted for a long time. It's hard to believe it was only fifty minutes."

Therapist: "That's pretty typical. It has to do with the altered state of consciousness you were experiencing. In this state, time can seem either sped up or slowed down."

lient: "How many sessions would it take to get through this?"

Therapist: "It's hard to say because it's so individual. Most clients seem to work through things in a range of five to ten MT sessions. MT can create profound changes in a fairly short time, sometimes even one session."

lient: "That's pretty fast...intriguing."

Therapist: "I'll agree with that. I've facilitated hundreds of MT sessions and I'm still impressed with how the Inner Source works."

lient: "I'm not sure I completely understand how it can work the way it does."

Therapist: "Understanding Meditative Therapy requires a shift in our viewpoint from linear and logical thinking which views the brain as a computer, to a more holistic approach which sees the brain as a hologram."

In the next chapter we'll explore the holographic paradigm which undergirds Meditative Therapy.

❖ *Key Points*

- The therapist accurately defines Meditative Therapy for selected clients, answers questions about the process, and provides a copy of *What   lients Want to Know About Meditative Therapy* (Appendix E), prior to beginning MT.

- The Inner Source process usually begins when clients close their eyes, formulate the intention for help, and watch and report whatever comes up.

- Although individuals respond uniquely to MT, therapeutic and creative goals are met though nine types of experiences.

- The therapist serves as a supportive guide, using minimal directives as needed to help clients enter, stay with or end the Inner Source process.

- The Inner Source process usually ends naturally and may signal an ending or simply stop generating material.

- The therapist records the MT session and provides a copy of this transcript to the client, debriefs the session, and remains available to clients in between sessions.

3

Paradigm and Perspective

This therapy is really strange. I've never had anything like it happen to me before. I feel very vulnerable. I'm trying to concentrate on trusting...just shut off all my fears and trust.

❖　　❖　　❖

That's so vivid, oh... That's a weird thing. Like these tingly feelings are over me, not in me. They start at the top and move to the bottom of me.

❖　　❖　　❖

The light is moving through my body from the outer edges to the center, taking my "me-ness" with it and leaving a huge, inflated shell that I am aware of, but not in. The light is getting brighter. It's moving backwards in time at a fast pace and I am being carried along with it.

❖　　❖　　❖

These passages, spoken spontaneously by clients during Meditative Therapy, illustrate the power of this wide-ranging holistic, inner-oriented process. Experiences of unusual depth and breadth dealing with mind, body, and spirit, arise naturally and purposefully during MT sessions.

Due to the innovative nature of Meditative Therapy, we would like to provide a present-day perspective of the paradigm shift currently affecting the   sciences, including psychology. This background material is a break from our task of presenting the practical aspects of MT. The following Buddhist koan may provide some incentive to stay with us on this brief, but important detour. "Before enlightenment I chopped wood and carried water. After enlightenment I chopped wood and carried water." In Chapter 4, we'll return to the practical task at hand, but by then you'll bring a new perspective to working with Meditative Therapy.

❖ A Psycho-Spiritual Synthesis

Lawrence LeShan, Ph.D., a psychotherapist best known for his work in mind-body medicine, predicts the integration of spiritual aspects into our profession. In his article, "The DSM 21: Introduction" published in *Advances, The Journal of Mind-Body Health* (1997), he conjectures that therapists of the twenty-first century will acknowledge

> The end of the idea that our field is an offshoot and a part only of medicine, and a new recognition that we have a second set of ancestors that have two separate, but interactive, functions.

This second set of ancestors, suggests LeShan, includes "the wise men and women of the tribe and the spiritual directors of organized religion." These ancestors have enjoined us with a dual legacy: to cure and to heal. The medical mission of curing directs us to help our clients overcome specific symptoms of disorders, described in the DSM IV. The spiritual mission of healing encourages us to help our clients "thrive" or reach their full potential. Increasingly, psychology recognizes the validity of both missions. For the practitioner, dealing with the constraints of managed care, which operates according to the standardized diagnostic system and time-limited services, honoring both of these missions becomes challenging, but not impossible.

❖ The Paradigm Partnership

> My barn having burned to the ground,
> I can now see the moon.
>
> — Taoist Sage

Meditative Therapy frequently generates unusual phenomena from an altered state of consciousness. Therefore, a comprehension of paradigms is crucial to understanding and accepting how MT operates.

Claire Cassidy, a consulting medical and nutritional anthropologist and director of research at the Traditional Acupuncture Institute in Maryland, defines paradigm as "the deep assumptions that undergird thinking and interpreting across whole segments of society" (Cassidy, 1994). Since these assumptions are deeply internalized, we often remain unaware of them, even though they formulate the basis of our view of reality. Paradigms are like barns: we put a lot of stock in them. When a new technique or method threatens to burn our barn, stampedes of resistance, defensiveness, and disbelief frequently result.

In the twentieth century, two paradigms, the *reductionist* and the *holistic,* inform our lives. The reductionist paradigm has dominated Western scientific thought until recently. Briefly, the reductionist approach categorizes things into component parts, which in our field results in the grouping together of various symptom constellations to form distinguishable and definable mental disorders. Understandably, the reductionist paradigm uses mechanical metaphors such as the "body-as-machine" and the "war-on-disease."

Reductionist thinking has permitted the research and development of vast resources for the application of psychoactive drugs and various treatment modalities to specific clients. However, such an approach also harbors some pitfalls, such as the tendency to reduce the person to the disorder, to relate to our clients from a hierarchical one-up position, and to see the completion of our work as the absence of disorder rather than increased holistic vitality (Cassidy, 1994).

The holistic paradigm seeks to comprehend wholeness. This paradigm informs much of Eastern thinking. Many holistic thinkers refer to Taoism, which recognizes the ultimate oneness or Tao of reality. Although parts are acknowledged, such as yin and yang, the yin and yang symbol points to an awareness of the balance and inter-relationship of the parts to the whole. Frequently, holism uses organic metaphors such as the "garden" and "natural growth" to convey the natural, self-healing methods of this approach.

Recently, the metaphor of the *hologram* has emerged as a graphic representation of the concept of oneness, which underlies holistic thinking. Holography records the wave field of light scattered by an object on a holographic plate, in what appears to be a meaningless swirl. Laser light can then regenerate the original wave pattern, creating a three-dimensional image. Significantly, any piece of the hologram can construct the entire image.

Holistic thinking allows us to see the client as a whole person, acknowledge each individual's uniqueness and relate to the client as a partner in healing. The emphasis on the interdependence of body, mind, and spirit opens our awareness to the effectiveness of methods that restore holistic balance, such as relaxation training, guided imagery, meditation, yoga, etc. (Cassidy, 1994). It has also stimulated new research and yielded new treatment approaches, such as Eye Movement Desensitization and Reprocessing and Meditative Therapy.

It might be desirable to see the moon without burning the barn. Cassidy suggests such a compromise: The "partnership perspective" emerges from the "Creative Third" where the argument over how to see reality dissipates into the simple awareness that reality just *is*. This allows alternative approaches and traditional methods to exist and to cooperate. (Cassidy, 1994). Applied to psychology, this partnership would allow the part access to the whole, and the whole access to the part. This approach integrates the best offerings of our medical ancestors with the best offerings of our spiritual ancestors.

❖ *The Holographic Universe and The Holographic Brain*

Historically, the discussions of science and spirituality have focused on their irreconcilable differences. However, the new advances in physics and neuro-science pave the way for greater compatibility and possible reconciliation. In the preface, we quote Carl Rogers' reference to a "new reality in which present, past, and future are intermingled, in which space is not a barrier and time has disappeared" (Rogers, 1973). He also suggests that interfacing this reality with the practice of therapy would bring excitement to the field of psychology.

Since ancient times, such a reality has been experienced through various mystical and spiritual practices. For the mystic, this reality is divine in nature. The recent contributions of David Bohm, a professor of theoretical physics and an expert in quantum theory from England, to quantum physics and Karl Pribram, professor of neuroscience at Stanford University, to neuro-science have opened western, scientific thinking to the mystic's spiritual reality. They also provide a background for the understanding of Meditative Therapy.

William Frost, Ph.D., professor of religious studies at the University of Dayton, explains Bohm's concept of the relationship between primordial reality and concrete reality.

According to Bohm, a primordial realm or "implicate order" precedes and underlies concrete reality or "explicate order." Quantum physicists refer to the explicate order as "unfolded" from another dimension, the implicate order. In this process, particular structures unfold from indefinite possibilities. The endless variety of living and non-living forms and inner and outer experiences attest to the limitless nature of this other dimension, the implicate order. All of concrete reality, the explicate order, is connected to the implicate order (Frost, 1997).

In a dialogue between Bohm and Renee Weber, professor of oriental studies at Rutgers University, Bohm observes that the implicate order communicates through display what must be done in order to manifest the explicate order, all that we know as reality (Bohm & Weber, 1982).

Bohm states that the brain acts similarly through the imagination. The metaphor of television conveys this idea simply. The television receiver picks up a signal and displays the content or meaning of the signal on the TV screen. Likewise, the brain picks up a signal from the implicate order and displays the meaning of this signal on the inner screen of the brain (Bohm & Wilber, 1982):

> *The complex chain of logical reasoning and its conclusions*
> *is displayed in an image which is an immediate guide to*
> *activity. This image is an outward display. If we ask what it*
> *is that is guided by this display, I say it can be nothing but*
> *the implicate. (Bohm & Wilber, 1982)*

Display also allows for feedback, the two-way communication between the implicate and explicate orders. The implicate order or some symbolization of it is displayed by human consciousness: consciousness in turn gives feedback to the implicate order. This allows the implicate order to "get to know itself better" and consciousness to "know itself more and more deeply, so it knows more of what it is doing" (Bohm & Wilber, 1982).

Karl Pribram's research furthers understanding of the brain, information processing, and consciousness. In "A New Perspective on Reality," Marilyn Fergusen (1982) explains that according to Pribram:

> *Information in the brain may be distributed as a hologram. The brain apparently has a parallel-processing capability that suggests a model-like optics, wherein connections are formed by paths traversed by light, in addition to its more limited digital or linear computer-type connections. A distribution pattern similar to that of a hologram also would explain how a specific memory does not have a location but is scattered throughout the brain (Fergusen, 1982).*

Interestingly, Pribram observes that the same circuits in the brain, centering on the amygdala, serve as the circuits for pathological disturbances, deja vu, and transcendental experience. The phenomena of altered consciousness or altered brain states may be due to an increased connection with the implicate order. Pribram hypothesizes that

> *This may enable interaction with reality at a primary level, thereby accounting for precognition, psychokinesis, healing, time distortion, rapid learning...and experience of "oneness with the universe." (Fergusen, 1982)*

❖ *Holography, Meditative Therapy, and the Inner Source*

Meditative Therapy, by accessing the Inner Source, puts client and therapist in touch with the implicate order described by Bohm and Pribram. As you'll see from many excerpts from MT transcripts, the work of the Inner Source could be described both as divine and as holographic, ideas which converge in Meditative Therapy. Karl Pribram offers this straightforward rationale: "The brain we know now allows for the experiences reported from spiritual disciplines" (Fergusen, 1982).

Metaphorically, the process of Meditative Therapy seems similar to holography: the Inner Source shines a concentrated beam of light on a particular point of consciousness, reveals its entirety, and displays meaning through holistic imaging.

Specifically, by closing the eyes and concentrating inwardly, the meaning of the implicate reality unfolds and becomes manifest in images, thoughts, feelings, and physical and spiritual sensations.

Let's look at some of the specific qualities of the Inner Source that resemble the implicate order:

1. The Inner Source is always present and constantly displaying.
2. The Inner Source is innate, self-healing, and self-unifying.
3. The Inner Source works through an individual consciousness.
4. The Inner Source works holistically, dealing with the whole person; mind, body and spirit.
5. The Inner Source is timeless — containing past, present and future — and may distort a "realistic" sense of time, compressing or expanding time as needed to do its healing work.
6. The Inner Source allows the possibility of rapid healing and rapid learning.
7. The Inner Source is therapeutic and provides a full range of experiences and methods to accomplish this goal.
8. The Inner Source can display unusual experiences such as precognition and out-of-body experiences.
9. The Inner Source can enhance a sense of oneness with the universe or a higher being.
10. The Inner Source is creative and stimulates positive growth towards increased consciousness and further unfolding.

This discussion of the new paradigm provides a background for understanding how Meditative Therapy works. However, whether or not we understand or accept this viewpoint, MT still works. As the "chop wood, carry water" koan says, we perform the same actions before and after enlightenment. The difference is in us, not in the nature of reality.

Meditative Therapy is best approached from a shift in perspective. It's difficult, if not impossible, to apply linear, logical thought, or cause-and-effect reasoning to a nonlinear dimension beyond time and space. Yet, it is also quite challenging to understand the holographic paradigm, with all its implications for brain processing through a holistic perspective. This leads us to join Karl Pribram in his admission: "I hope you realize that I don't understand any of this" (Fergusen, 1982).

That said, we invite you to "suspend disbelief" as we return to our discussion of the "nuts and bolts" of Meditative Therapy.

Key Points

- Meditative Therapy synthesizes scientific and spiritual approaches to healing and curing.

- The holographic paradigm provides a working hypothesis for understanding the Inner Source process: MT stimulates holographic brain information processing, which is capable of communicating with implicate reality.

- The Inner Source process, due to its communication with implicate reality, can create holistic, individualistic, unusual and rapid treatment effects, unlimited by the ordinary constraints of reality, such as time.

4 ❖

Meditative Therapy, A Holistic Approach

I feel like a puppet. Strings are attached to my big toes and elbows, my head, my middle. They have control of my tongue too. I'm being pulled on strings, I'm dancing. I don't like being controlled.

❖   ❖   ❖

I'm seeing myself wearing a coat. No one can see inside. I keep it on so I don't have to deal with anything. I realize that is what I do with everything in my whole life. I get away from people.

❖   ❖   ❖

I see both of us standing, facing each other. I'm feeling a lot of sadness on both of our sides. We're losing the old parts — the old way we used to be...(tears)...I'm changing so much...the person I used to be is dead.

❖   ❖   ❖

The above excerpts from MT sessions may seem familiar to therapists regardless of orientation. The language of metaphor, the insight into a defense mechanism, or the expression of feelings all occur regularly within various therapeutic approaches. These responses illustrate the integrative nature of Meditative Therapy. The analysis of many transcripts illustrates the breadth of techniques occurring in Meditative Therapy experiences. However diverse, the unifying theory of the holistic approach explains the tremendous variety of MT experiences.

❖ *Meditative Therapy in the Therapeutic Universe*

Because Meditative Therapy deals with the whole person, psychologically, physically, and spiritually, it naturally fits within the holistic theoretical orientation. According to Frank Nugent's *Introduction to the Profession of ounseling* (1994), this orientation acknowledges the interconnectedness of the body, mind, and spirit. MT works to create greater balance and unity within each person.

Nugent uses five categories to organize the various theories of counseling: *human nature, sources of maladaptive behavior, counseling goals, counseling techniques,* and *counseling relationship.* MT shares some attributes with several other theoretical approaches, and our definition of this holistic therapy is refined by viewing MT in the context of each of Nugent's categories:

Human Nature: As in Holistic Theory, MT holds that body, mind and spirit are interconnected and in harmony with the world and the cosmos. More specifically, MT recognizes that each person has innate evolutionary inner processes that unfold naturally through holistic pathways, leading toward self-healing and transformation. MT refers to this process as the Inner Source. In addition, inherent higher-level potentialities exist, and can be tapped into or allowed to develop. This self-healing potential is also in keeping with the client-centered view of self-actualization and the Jungian emphasis on individuation. The self evolves through greater awareness and integration of the soul.

Sources of Maladaptive Behavior: MT recognizes the multiple sources of maladaptive behavior posited by various theories. In general, life experiences — psychological, physiological, and spiritual — may cause disturbances that remain unresolved and need to be processed. These disturbances could reflect the rational emotive and cognitive-behavioral view of inaccurate perceptions, distorted reasoning and destructive self-talk, or the gestalt belief of an individual's conflict between inner needs and outer demands. In fact, an analysis of any one MT transcript might lead to the belief that MT fits within existential or psychoanalytic theory.

Since MT individualizes treatment to client needs, it is highly integrative, drawing on various theories as needed. However, it shares the holistic belief that these disturbances, regardless of source, result in a *disconnection or imbalance of body, mind and spirit*, resulting in a lack of unity of the self and disassociation from the world.

Counseling Goals: Similarly to holistic theory, MT seeks to restore unity and create greater balance between body, mind, and spirit. MT believes that effective psychotherapy allows natural healing and growth processes to unfold, develops awareness of inner and outer issues, and uses both therapeutic experience and insight to facilitate life changes. Meditative Therapy may address current life issues, long-term/recurrent emotional problems, and/or growth toward self-fulfillment. In this process, MT's integrative qualities become apparent, often incorporating goals from various theoretical orientations. In order to achieve greater unity of the self, some individuals may need to correct inaccurate perceptions, while other clients may seek to become more authentic in relationships with others.

Counseling Techniques: MT techniques focus on educating the client regarding MT, supporting the process of MT, and furthering the integration of MT material into the client's conscious, waking life.

Counseling Relationship: In any psychotherapeutic relationship the therapist must first establish a truthful, open relationship built on empathy, positive regard, and trust. Without this relationship, most clients will not be open to change, much less to engage in a new experience that involves an altered state of consciousness. Such a therapeutic relationship helps the client feel safe, trust the therapist, and allow the free flow of meditative experience. Truthfulness is a two-way street, of course, and the therapist must educate the client regarding the nature of MT and discuss the possibility of abreaction and other powerful emotional experiences. Since informed consent is an ethical — and often legal — requirement in psychotherapy, use of a form such as that in Appendix G is highly recommended.

During MT sessions, the meditative therapist remains relatively non-directive, supportive and empathetic, guiding and encouraging the client to be patient with and accepting of the Inner Source process. The client's perception of the therapist's presence offers support during more intense abreactive sequences. One client's comment echoed this sentiment: "You were right there with me. I felt the connection. We were sharing this at a very deep level."

Following MT, the therapist assumes a variety of roles, depending on the client's issues and needs. We recommend a follow-up call after the first MT session for all clients. We also call clients after sessions that produce abreaction to ensure that the client has returned to normal functioning, and to allow the therapist to initiate an interim session if needed.

In every sense, the MT therapist must be a highly skilled, creative, and integrative clinician.

❖ ## Meditative Therapy Client Characteristics

In developing Meditative Therapy, we have worked with a wide variety of individuals. The following categories briefly describe the population:

Age: The majority of MT clients ranged between 18 and 70 years, with a median of about *27*.

Diagnoses: In terms of the DSM IV, MT was used to treat disorders of mood, anxiety, and adjustment. PTSD, due to wartime experience and childhood abuse, responded favorably to Meditative Therapy. MT also proved effective with a variety of V codes: Relational Problems, problems related to abuse or neglect and bereavement, academic, occupational, identity, religious or spiritual and phase of life problems.

Ethnicity: MT has been used with clients of Euro-American, Hispanic, Asian, and Middle Eastern cultural backgrounds. The data for MT with multicultural clients is limited to just ten individuals.

Socioeconomic Status: MT clients fit into a normal socioeconomic curve, the majority being from the middle range.

Since MT utilizes the client's natural, self-healing ability, we believe that MT will prove helpful regardless of age, cultural background, and socioeconomic status. However, within this population, the therapist will discover some clients who do not respond well to MT or prefer other therapeutic approaches. A poor response to MT usually stems from a given client's inability to trust the flow of meditative experiences. This situation may be improved by further clarification of the process and encouragement or coaching during MT.

❖ *Further Considerations for the Use of MT*

Client response: To determine the effectiveness of MT for each individual, the therapist must *observe* the client's response during and after MT sessions and *ask* for the client's reactions to the therapy. Various approaches to enhance MT in these situations are explained in Chapter 10. Occasionally, however, the process may be working but the client prefers another therapeutic approach. In this case, it is important to honor client preferences.

Therapist training and expertise: The practice of psychotherapy in any modality requires an appropriate background of professional training, supervised clinical experience, and adherence to legal and ethical standards (e.g., licensure, professional ethics). Moreover, therapists should use MT only with clients whom they are qualified and trained to treat. Meditative Therapy is not a cure-all or substitute for clinical competence, training, or judgment.

Client strengths and resources: Since MT entails deeper involvement with inner material, the therapist should consider the client's current situation prior to beginning MT. It's important to assess the client's availability for therapy, inner resources for dealing with emotionally charged material, and outer support systems. If necessary, MT should be delayed until the client's schedule permits adequate time for therapy. Appointments should be scheduled to allow clients time to rest or relax before returning to work, etc. At times positive coping skills and outer support systems should be enhanced prior to beginning MT.

❖ *Contraindications for Meditative Therapy*

Through the practice and research of MT, we have observed contraindications that stem from the nature of Meditative Therapy. Although MT is a natural therapy, based on a self-healing, self-unifying process, certain cautions should be observed. First of all, MT can facilitate abreaction, extended discharging which may involve experiences of intense emotional states, and/or physical reactions. (These experiences are described in more detail in Chapter 5.) Secondly, clients may experience greater vulnerability outside of the session due to increased contact and awareness of their inner material. Spontaneous abreactions, disturbing dreams, enhanced emotional states, and increased memories may all occur. MT contraindications mostly stem from these two possibilities and necessitate further exploration of the following considerations.

History: A history of repeated hospitalizations for psychotic episodes, suicide attempts, or substance abuse indicates the need to evaluate the client's current status carefully and proceed cautiously. These occurrences may suggest the absence of the inner or outer resources needed to proceed with MT.

Previous Therapy: A history of many therapists may indicate poor ability to develop and maintain a relationship with the therapist. Again, MT should only be used within the context of a trusting, open relationship.

Diagnoses: Clients with the following disorders should not receive treatment with MT: active substance abuse, dissociative disorders and dementias, psychotic disorders and personality disorders.

Medical Conditions: A complete medical history should be obtained prior to beginning Meditative Therapy. Clients who have a severe health condition, which may compromise their ability to withstand abreactive sequences, should not undergo MT. Medical conditions such as diabetes, heart disease, lupus, fibromyalgia, neurological disorders, pregnancy, or any other individual or collective conditions, which may put the client at risk during or after MT, should be avoided. This decision is partly based on W. Luthe's contraindications in reference to Autogenic

Training. (Luthe, 1969). In these cases, the client's system is already compromised and the stress of MT may worsen the medical condition. When in doubt, the therapist should err on the side of caution and use other therapeutic modalities. More research needs to be conducted in this area.

Although these considerations may seem highly cautious, they fall within current ethical guidelines and standards of care. The Meditative Therapist must be especially aware of these parameters, until MT receives greater research and widespread usage. It is hoped that future research will establish precise guidelines for the use of Meditative Therapy.

❖ ### *Benefits of Meditative Therapy*

To close this chapter, let's look at a few of the benefits of Meditative Therapy.

Short-Term: Most clients will significantly reduce presenting complaints within five to ten sessions of sixty to ninety minutes.

Person-Centered: Since MT trusts inner processing and allows the natural flow of inner experiences with minimal interpretation, it is centered on and respectful of the person.

Diagnostically Vital: MT is an integrative therapist's dream. MT uncovers faulty cognitions and belief systems, traumatic experiences, phobias, and emotional states related to the client's problem, allowing the therapist to gain a more thorough psychological picture of the client's life.

Holistic: MT accesses the full range of response within each person. Psychological, physiological, and spiritual experiences frequently occur during MT. Most therapies do not have this capability of treating the whole person.

Inner Source Directed: Engaging in MT allows a higher part of each individual's consciousness to guide the therapy. The Inner Source is inherently spiritual, though some may prefer the terms inner intelligence or biological wisdom. This process occurs naturally: The Inner Source provides the healing and creative experiences necessary for each individual.

As you proceed through the book, we're certain that you won't be disappointed. You will witness the full range of power, beauty, and healing available within, to all who are willing to enter. As Rene Daumal stated, "The door to the invisible must be visible."

❖ *Key Points*

- Meditative Therapy fits within the holistic theoretical orientation, valuing the interconnectedness of body, mind, and spirit.

- Meditative Therapy accesses an innate Inner Source process that unfolds naturally through holistic pathways, leading toward self-healing and transformation.

- The MT process individualizes treatment needs and utilizes integrative methods to accomplish these goals.

- A positive therapeutic relationship, based on empathy, mutual regard, and trust must be established prior to proceeding with MT.

- Although MT is effective with a wide variety of disorders and V codes, the therapist must screen for factors that may put the client at risk, such as psychotic disorders, dissociative disorders, active substance abuse, and severe medical conditions.

- Some of the benefits of Meditative Therapy include the following: short-term, person-centered, diagnostically vital, holistic, and Inner Source directed.

5

Therapeutic Experiences in Meditative Therapy

> *What did these people do in order to achieve the development*
> *that liberated them? As far as I could see they did nothing,*
> *wu wei (action through no-action), but let things happen. As*
> *Master Lu-tsu teaches in our text, the light rotates according*
> *to its own law, if one does not give up one's ordinary*
> *occupation. The art of letting things happen, action through*
> *non-action, letting go of oneself, as taught by Meister*
> *Eckhaart, became for me the key opening the door to the way.*
> *We must be able to let things happen in the psyche.*
>
> — C. G. Jung

❖   ❖   ❖

The two basic goals of Meditative Therapy consist of a therapeutic (healing) goal and a creative goal. This chapter examines therapeutic experiences in MT; the creative dimension is explored in Chapter 6.

The therapeutic process takes place more frequently in Meditative Therapy. It can be analyzed in terms of six categories: discharging, extended discharging, abreaction, treatment, understanding, and reinforcement. Seeing how the Inner Source works within each of these categories enhances an appreciation of the process. Any one session may make use of several of these methods in varying combinations. Figure 5-1 lists the frequency of occurrence of each of these six therapeutic categories. These short segments are taken from longer MT transcripts for purposes of illustration. Therefore, in these examples, the overall integrity of a complete session may not be apparent.

Figure 5-1	The Therapeutic Journey of the Inner Source Based on 100 Participants*

The Therapeutic Healing Goal

Category	Percentage Occurance
1. Discharging	100%
2. Extended Discharging	95%
3. Reinforcement	75%
4. Understanding	71%
5. Abreaction	20%

* The 100 persons included here represent my entire poluation of Meditative Therapy clients at the date of this writing. Other samples noted in this book are drawn from this group of 100.

❖ *The Therapeutic (Healing) Goal of Meditative Therapy*

The Inner Source employs a variety of means to help the individual overcome psychological, physiological and spiritual difficulties:

1. Discharging: Experiencing momentary visual images, bodily reactions, thoughts, and feelings.
Examples: seeing colors and patterns, smelling odors, twitching, feeling cold, feeling anxious, and visualizing people, places, events, etc.

2. Extended Discharging: Experiencing longer sequences of visual images, bodily reactions, thoughts, and feelings, but without abreactive intensity.
Examples: seeing a series of images from childhood, thinking about a relationship with a partner, feeling physical responses from a past illness, etc.

3. Abreaction: Reliving or re-experiencing various portions of disturbing or traumatic events.
Examples: reliving Vietnam combat experiences, the death of a loved one, or a sexual assault and experiencing the physical sensations and emotions associated with these experiences.

4. Treatment: An integrative array of techniques designed to alleviate symptoms.

Examples: desensitization, cognitive restructuring, pointing out defenses, etc.

5. Understanding: Realizing the causes of one's difficulties, gaining insights, or arriving at solutions to confusing problem areas.

Examples: connecting the present problem with a past physical injury or emotional upset, coming to new conclusions about one's upbringing, and gaining personal insights about the meaning of life and/or how to live.

6. Reinforcement: Gaining a rewarding psychological, physical, or spiritual feeling during the Meditative Therapy process.

Examples: seeing a beautiful or relaxing scene, feeling deeply relaxed, feeling exhilarated, experiencing a humorous incident, and having a "peak" experience.

Discharging, extended discharging, and abreaction form a continuum of physical, mental, emotional and/or spiritual release from brief to extensive. Discharging, with momentary responses, usually takes place at the beginning of the session. As the session progresses, discharging often evolves into extended discharging and abreaction. These responses correspond to similar reactions in concentrative and mindfulness meditation and are naturally healing. Neuro-physiological research and meditation research regards discharging as stress release from the nervous system. These homeostatic responses help the system self-regulate. Numerous research studies on meditation and Autogenic Training demonstrate the holistic benefits of discharging.

The balance of this chapter is devoted to case examples of therapeutic experiences.

❖ *Discharging*

The following MT excerpts illustrate the variety of holistic responses that occur during discharging.

1. Physical sensations:
Feel pretty relaxed, some twitching in my thumb. My stomach feels a little tight. I feel a little dizzy. Feels like I'm being pushed from

behind, some pressure underneath my back. Muscles in forearms are tense. Muscles under my eyes are a little tight.

2.   Visual images and physical sensations:
Mostly images flitting past: "V" shapes, orange and yellow fire in the middle. A headache on the lower part of my head came with it. It's gone. I feel if I let go of my hands, my middle will peel off on both sides.

3.   Emotional release:
The closest to freedom that I can get is laughter. No guilt when I'm exhilarated. Laughter, just feeling like laughing (laughs). *Don't know why* (laughs). *I used to do that when I was little, just giggling* (laughs).

❖❖ **Extended Discharging: Physical Events**

1. Broken Bones: This man had broken his right leg twice and his left leg once. A surgical pin had been inserted into his right leg.
I guess my right leg is going to hurt this morning, the one I had surgery on. It sure hurts now. I just had a visual picture of just when I broke it. I skied down on it without assistance and went for two days on it and didn't know it was broken.

2. Dental Work: This man had undergone many hours of dental work.
My forehead feels smooth, but my head feels heavy and numb. I have a headache way down inside. My jaw is real sore, like a dentist has been working on me. God knows I've had enough of that work done. I still have that headache and my jaw aches and my whole mouth. Now I don't feel so relaxed, I'm anxious. Feels kind of like just before I go to the dentist. I'm hot and sweaty and my palms are sweaty.

3. Polio: This woman had polio as a child.
I feel a real rush now and feel a little afraid. I keep seeing the house (she describes it). *I feel energy going out of my arms and out of my head. I see myself when I was sick. My neck really hurts between my shoulder blades and I can see me soaking in the tub when I was sick. I felt a big rush in my body, almost like a gas. I see the backyard and an adult and kid. Kid being carried;*

*kid is sick. I see the tub when I was sick with polio. My back is
stiff. I feel an awful lot of weird energy in my body, like it's
uncomfortable. Makes me feel kind of stiff and achy. I feel that
energy or whatever all over, like I'm about to start shaking from
being cold.*

Extended Discharging: Psychological Events

1. High School Experiences: This man revisited school
experiences which took place seven years before.

> *I didn't drink much from then until high school, then it took a
> new meaning for me. We'd have a 6-pack stashed in the woods.
> Go out and freeze and drink then go back to the basketball game.
> It took the whole week to line up the 6-pack* (laughs). *One time
> we had a big party and got malt liquor and beer and everyone
> else had gone home. We stayed the night to party, but one of us
> got separated and later two got caught in the recreation room
> and the priests kept telling us they thought more were involved.
> Later we sat on the hill, pretty drunk, concrete stairs and a priest
> started coming up. I got so scared, my whole body was wired and
> I vomited* (stomach gurgles). *Not because I was sick, but because
> I might get caught. I was really terrified. Wasn't our Priest
> though and we all got to graduate* (gurgles).

2. Divorce: This woman had married at an early age, then
divorced after several years. The divorce had taken place ten years
ago and she believed that it no longer bothered her.

> *Boy, getting married at sixteen is the worst thing of all.
> I would have nightmares at night about my first marriage up
> until I got married the second time. It was the worst thing that
> ever happened. He would criticize me for everything I said and
> did; I could do nothing right. Yet, before we were married the
> things I did seemed O.K. There was no way I could be myself.
> R* (present husband) *blames me for being married before.
> I shouldn't be, there is no way I should be punished. Basically,
> those last two years we weren't married anyway* (dry crying —
> making noises and motions as in crying, but without tears). *We
> only had intercourse three times and I got pregnant. I feel like
> I've paid enough, suffered enough, for being married before. It
> shouldn't matter anymore* (breathing heavily). *I would cry and*

cry, and I lost 15 pounds in less than a year. Our first child was 10 days old before he saw it. It's terrible being pregnant and having a baby with a person who's resisting.

❖ Abreaction: Physical Events

1. Doctor Visits: This fifty-year-old woman re-experienced visits to the doctor as a young child for a urinary disorder. The visits required dilation of the urethra.

> *I want to scream, but I can't, I never can. Even in my dreams, I can never scream. Sometimes I wake up at night and scream, but not really. My throat closes off and I know I've been trying to scream because I'm* (breathing quickens) — *I feel like I'm being held down* (stomach gurgles). (Starts crying) *I feel like I'm being held down in that room. Oh God, I'm in that doctor's office! All these people, and my mother's there and I'm on this table and it's hard like the floor. Oh, God* (gurgles, sobbing)*! I can't even see it! I'm so ashamed! Put my feet in the stirrups, I can't believe it, and my mother was standing there. Everyone was white. Oh God. Told me to relax, that it wouldn't hurt. I hate them, I hate them. I think I'd kill them now. I don't want to kill, but I feel like it. How could Mother have stood there and watched that? Why didn't she pick me up and hold me? I don't know, maybe when kids are six you don't hold them anymore.*

2. Childhood Disease: This twenty-six-year-old man had a bone disorder, Osgood-Schlatter disease, as a child.

> *My body feels crooked, doesn't feel aligned right. I don't feel straight. I'm aware of a pain in my left leg, muscles are twitching a little bit, tightening and loosening. I don't feel sad, but I have the feeling about sadness. My leg's still doing it — still doing it. It's shaking* (very observable). *Calming down, real soft twitching, boom, boom-boom, boom-boom, boom. It's getting harder and faster now, very vigorous, boom, boom! It's shaking from side to side.*

3. Miscarriage: This young woman had lost a baby several years before due to a miscarriage. (Obviously miscarriage is both a physical and a psychological event.)

Color is like a spinning wheel, like fans you used to get when you were a kid, on a stick (starts sobbing & coughing). *Oh, I don't understand that. We used to run with them* (stops crying and starts crying). *I just feel sad. I just feel sad* (deep breath). *Baffles me about — I don't even know the name of —* (stops crying). *My side still hurts and stomach still gurgles* (sobbing again). *I just don't feel like crying. Oh, oh,* (stops sobbing) *— saw just white all around my eyes. My side is still hurting some. I just feel tired, not tired, just — I don't know, maybe kind of just accepting it* (crying), *just accepting it. Oh,* (sits up and cries) *I can't cry lying down. I feel like rocking back and forth* (rocks from side-to-side and around). *I want something to hold; I wanted that baby! I wanted that baby!* (sobbing and rocking — lies down — strokes and rubs her hair — still sobbing) *Oh, I guess, I'm feeling like, the baby is beside me* (crying), *I don't know, I don't know. Hal* (husband) *didn't know how much I appreciated him. He didn't know it was real. He didn't know it. I just feel like a whole square of hurt just moved away. I can't have it anyway. Oh,* (sighs) *feeling cold again and can't* (crying stops) *keep thoughts about that all the time —* (whispering...laughs). *I don't feel anything, except cold* (shivers again). *There's something covering my eyes, nothing else going on. Just as I said that I felt my heart beating very heavily. Aware now that my head hurts* (deep breathing). *Sometimes my mind really makes me mad. I feel like I'm fighting myself. Right shoulder is tight, right side aches* (shakes her head). *I guess I didn't know that hurts* (crying). *She asked me how old the child was* (sobbing). *You can say things in your mind and that's O.K. and accept it, but that doesn't mean it's past* (stops crying). *I feel good — don't feel bad. I really feel tired and I feel like going to sleep.* (End of session).

Abreaction: Psychological Events

1. Relationship with Father: A twenty-eight-year-old woman in her first session revisits her past relationship with her father.

Now I feel sad, not like striking at him, just feel sad. I've not done anything, but he doesn't seem to like me. No matter how hard I try, it's never enough. I can do well in school, but it doesn't matter. Daddy — I like school. That's not enough —

school's not enough (sobbing). *Makes me feel angry. He won't tell me why. He won't tell me how to fix it. I just wish you'd tell me why you don't like me* (sobbing). *I've always tried to do what you wanted, but it's never been — if he would just tell me why, I'd feel better. I just can't bear not knowing why you don't like me.*

2. Suicide of Father: This young woman's alcoholic father committed suicide when she was in her early teens. During the year following his death, she gained 100 pounds. She had never talked about this experience. Although she didn't express strong emotional or physical reactions, her voice became very intense and her inner experience was obviously very powerful.

I'm looking into a broken mirror and I'm screaming. I feel as if there is a steel band around my chest. What I'm seeing upsets me a lot. I've never talked about it before. ("It's okay to talk about it.") *I'm in a room where father killed himself and I feel really sick. I feel really upset because there are small pieces of brain on the walls. I remember thinking I should do something about it because I was worried about my brother coming down, but I couldn't. So I went upstairs and got in bed and sort of curled up around this very bad feeling. Now I'm seeing my father sitting in a deep blue chair in the living room and I'm there watching TV. And I feel, not exactly frightened, but apprehensive, like I might be scared. When I sit next to my father, I always pull back a little. He's eating chocolate and drinking coke. When he sits there, he looks very small and lonely. Whenever he drinks coke and eats chocolate, he's not as frightening: He seems less large. It's hard to explain, but I can't tell when I'm frightened of father. His eyes get fierce and kind of wild and he does crazy things.*

❖ Integrative Treatment

The Inner Source is naturally integrative: It employs a wide variety of techniques from different theoretical orientations. The following examples illustrate some of the most frequent treatment techniques, but the MT therapist will encounter an endless variety of methods with different clients over the years. Not all techniques will be evident in one session or with one individual. These examples are taken from many different client transcripts. They also represent short sequences within the longer Meditative Therapy session.

1. Behavioral Therapy — Systematic Desensitization: Janis found her father dead in his chair in her living room, three months after he had moved in with her. Six months later, she was bothered by intrusive images of his death. When she thought of him or walked by that corner of the room, she visualized him as he was when she found him dead.

I'm seeing Dad sitting in the chair, alive, petting the dogs. Now he's dead, head on his chest, like when I found him. Now he's alive, smiling. He loved the dogs. Now dead. It's alternating back and forth. Dead — alive. Dead — alive. Dead — alive. It just keeps alternating. On — off. On — off. (This sequence lasted about eight minutes.) *The images are just fading into one, just peaceful. Sitting there, a smile on his face.*

After this session, the intrusive image no longer bothered her and she was able to remember a full range of images of her father when he was alive.

2. Use of metaphor: Carol had difficulty saying no to requests. Typically, she gave in and found much of her time taken up by doing favors for friends and spending hours on the phone listening to their problems. She often felt overwhelmed and resentful when her needs were neglected in the process.

I haven't talked to P. in two years. Yet she calls. I'm this rock. I'm tired of it. They think, "She's together, she can take it." Inside I'm falling apart. Tired, dragged down. I'm in the ocean, a tiny island jutting out of the water. I'm just barely keeping my head above water. It would be easy for a couple of waves to come crashing along. I'd disappear. I'm trying to turn the ocean away — make the tide flow out. See the water creeping out. Feel like I've gotten rid of stuff. It threatens to come back and drown me. Go away. Be out there. They can be their own rocks. They have the same tools I do. I just take advantage of them. I'm feeling determined.

After this session Carol commented, "I used to feel selfish if I refused a request or didn't feel like listening to someone. That's less of a problem now."

3. Psychoanalytic — *relationship of present to childhood events:* Patricia was feeling depressed at Christmas. The sequence of associations led back to her childhood memories and helped her release the fear and anger associated with the holidays.

> *Body feels like I can't breathe. Holidays aren't important. I don't want them to be important. Bogs me down. Too much thinking. I get overwhelmed. I don't really want to celebrate, even with my family. After everything is finished, have to put pieces back together. Living at home, when I was growing up, I had to remove myself. Dad would throw plates of food at the wall. Everybody got up and cleaned it up. I don't know if Dad stayed there. Pretty scared, not knowing what to do. A real cold feeling towards my parents. My dad was too dangerous to be around. I had to be cautious, never know what would happen next. I associate my Dad with holidays. All the stuff my mother had to go through. She wasted her life taking care of him. Sometimes I feel like I'm wasting my life — looking at the bad stuff. To be in the present is hard. Everyone else is joyful. I'm upset.*

After this session, Patricia was able to have a Christmas dinner with her two grown daughters. For the first time, she decided not to include her ex-husband. At the next session she reported that "I just decided that I didn't have to feel joyful. It was okay to be sad. I even shared my feelings with L. and K. (daughters) and that felt good. I felt closer to them. That was probably the best Christmas I've ever had."

4. Psychodynamic: Brian felt out of control due to his compulsive eating. The following sequence helped him understand the relationship between his current behavior and past unmet emotional needs from his father.

> *Feeling of being heavy. Image of me at the fridge at night, feeling embarrassed even telling you about this. I'm sneaking. If Beth (wife) got up and saw me I'd feel embarrassed. I'm seeing an image of an exaggerated self, big, like Dad. I have a feeling*

*of not wanting to be like him. He eats anything, all the time.
He's out of control in lots of ways — alcohol — a fly-by-the-
seat-of-your-pants kind of guy. I'm saying, "I don't want to be
like you." Feeling really uncomfortable with my own behavior.
Sadness about Dad not being there. Feeling sad. Dad just
wasn't there. A terrible sadness.*

Later in the session, Brian recalled that his father would
periodically abandon the family. He realized that when his father
was absent, there frequently was not enough money for food. He
remembered when he was five, opening the cabinet and finding
only a few cans of soup.

5. Psychoanalytic, Jungian — exploration of an archetype: Ann,
a nurse and mother of two children, struggles with meeting her
family's needs. She often feels that she can't get her own needs
met, or that it would be selfish to make this a priority. In this
session, she identified with the martyr archetype.

*I'm on the cross. I feel teary, sensation in my hands, feet —
the weight of breathing. I can see people down below, laughing,
jeering, also some sadness and tears. Seems very hot, my mouth is
dry. Humiliating to be exposed on a cross in front of everybody.
Seems like I've been here forever. I'm beginning to wonder...will
there be an end to the suffering? I can understand why Jesus said,
"Why hast Thou forsaken me?" Have I been forgotten? Another
sharp pain in my side. The pain is becoming so much that I'm
going to another space.*

The session continued to explore the death of Christ, his burial
and his resurrection. After this session, Ann said, "I never realized
how completely I had identified with this story from the time I was
a little child. When I was in grade school and other kids made fun
of me, I felt grateful that I was saving others from their taunts."
She concluded that maybe it was time to "come off the cross."

6. Psychoanalytic, Jungian — exploration of the shadow: Dave, a
history professor, fears asserting himself with his wife. In this
sequence, he confronts his fear of his shadow side that prevents
him from speaking up.

When she got depressed, she went out and bought this hideous antique chair. It was really expensive. I thought, "You went out and that without discussing it with me." I'm earning all the money. Feels resentful. I'm keeping it in. My chest is tight, heavy. I thought, she's depressed, so don't kick a person when they're down. She might leave me. A male friend of mine would have said, "This is stupid. Take it back." See myself taking it and throwing it, breaking it into smithereens. The shadow part. Not sure I'm right about this. I know if there were a God who observed the chair incident, he'd say "You're correct. She shouldn't have bought the chair." I could say it politely. "I really don't like the chair. I'd like you to return it." It might turn into an argument. I'd feel worse then. Tension. I might push it to the limit. I'm afraid of going over the limit. I might say something hurtful. She might leave. Ultimately, I'll get hurt worse. I stuff the feeling. I think about talking about it later, but I never do.

This session marked a turning point in Dave's ability to acknowledge his feelings and see the validity of his viewpoint. He later worked on developing assertiveness skills.

7. Gestalt — conflict of inner needs and outer demands: In this sequence, Gina struggles with the decision whether to have her aging parents move in with her. She has been the family caretaker up until now.

Feeling in the top of my head. Something else is controlling me. Scary thing. If I come face to face with it, I don't know if I'll like seeing it. Image of my parents. I'm afraid I'll get so angry with them that I'll have to abandon them. That would hurt my mother so much. They've mortgaged my life with so many foolish business moves. I'll have to take care of them. But I'll resent taking care of them. My brother won't take care of them. He'll hide his head in the sand, allow me to take care of them. If I don't take care of them, I'll lose the entire family. That would put me completely alone in the world. I don't know how to deal with that. I could move into the cottage in back, put my parents in the front house. I could see myself not having a life. Like the movie Like Water for Chocolate.

This session helped Gina become aware of the price of having her parents move into her house. She decided against this and her parents found a rental close to their old neighborhood. Once she shifted her focus to her own life, she began dating and a year later became engaged.

8. Gestalt — *dialogue with a disowned part of the self:* Mike felt like an outsider with his wife and two teenage daughters. In this session, he contacts a softer, more open side of himself.

> *Go back to the little boy. He's reaching out for some healing or something* (sobbing). *See the little boy and the big me standing there together, both in the same place. Not knowing what to do — very scared. Seems like we're both waiting for something to happen. We're both looking to each other. Pain way down inside* (rubs chest). *Feels like a need for warmth, a need for a home* (sobbing). *The big guy wants to hold the little guy, but he can't get there. Seems bright to me. The little guy feels like he's saying something. The big guy is not so sure. The word "trust" is coming through. The little guy is saying, "Got to trust in your heart, can't shut down." Feels like the little guy wants to hang around* (deep breath). *Seems to be where they both come to. Both realize the heart. That's where the focus has to be.*

In a later marital session, his wife reported that Mike had been able to talk to his daughters when problems occurred, instead of yelling at them.

9. Gestalt — *confronting a secret:* Tom, a thirty-nine-year-old accountant, had been imprisoned in Guatemala when he was twenty-one. He had never told anyone about the experience. This sequence confronts him with his past.

> *I'm hearing, "You can wear a facade." Something comforting about that — not being exposed. Maybe I'm hiding something. Jail. A feeling I had when I was there. Frustration of being cooped up, a small dormitory with forty guys — an array of characters — revolutionary guys from Central America.*

After this session, Tom found the courage to tell his fiancee about his past. He was very relieved when she didn't reject him.

10. *Existential — finding meaning:* This same man's MT session helps him make peace with his past by finding meaning in his incarceration.

> *I had a short wave radio. Listened to the Voice of America from Moscow. The whole world was focused in that jail cell. I was doing Yoga, reading. I realized I could write. Wrote a lot of letters to people. This is how I developed. Before then, scared to go to college — terrified about writing. Such a change. I was almost empowered by being there. Image of a birth — I'm being reborn. Strong, powerful. It's a transformation. Exercising, Yoga — a metamorphosis — intellectual, physical, a spiritual journey. Myself and these changes. I'm more proud of that change than I am of my graduation from college. I took on a challenge. I survived that.*

The above two sessions, which dealt primarily with prison, helped reduce Tom's feelings of stigma and isolation regarding this experience. His heightened sense of self-esteem and acceptance increased his confidence in interpersonal relationships.

11. *Existential — striving for authentic identity:* Raised in a large Catholic family, Deborah helped raise her seven brothers and sisters. Her own sense of identity became submerged in order to be the good girl and receive parental praise. She came into therapy to "find herself."

> *I'm aware of a physical sensation that goes all the way around my trunk. It's fear, fear of being found out and judged, fear of bringing something up. I'm trying to keep myself contained and kept together in this mold of my body. The body never feels quite right, because so much, everything has to be kept in, contained. Thinking of how my sister and her husband communicate. He can ask questions, she can too. Sadness. If I had asked a question, I wouldn't have gotten past one, because it's not okay. Loss of what I haven't had. Difficult for me to disclose or expose myself without wondering what the other person thinks about me. I can feel a lot of tightness just now. I might shatter if I didn't hold everything in so tightly. It's like I have wire wrapped around me. I'm afraid if I don't wear tight clothes, I'll just get bigger. That's been unacceptable. The family message is "You have to stay small."*

> *I'm going to see my family this week — keep myself contained the whole time. I don't want to. I don't want to care if*

they want to judge me. Seems like caring about this...it's the child that cares. She still wants approval from everybody.

She later reported that her visit with her family had been very different. She had actually enjoyed the time and reported feeling less "hooked in by the family games."

12. *Existential — accepting death of an old part of the self:* Kristin, thirty-nine, came to therapy due to generalized anxiety and panic disorder. Her personal changes of greater self-reliance, responsibility, and assertiveness impacted her marriage, which also improved significantly.

I feel I'm changing so much, that the person I used to be is dead. It's hard to figure out how to act or react. I see both of us standing facing each other, not real close, but holding hands. Feeling a lot of sadness on both our sides. We're losing the old parts, the old way we used to be.

Prior to Kristin's therapy, she took a passive role, relying on her husband to take care of her. This session shows her in transition, struggling to find a new way of being. Subsequently, she took over the maintenance of her own car, which helped alleviate her anxiety about driving and being away from home. This enabled her to drive six hours to attend a workshop. Her car broke down on the trip, but she was able to deal with the situation without having a panic attack. Presently, she is thinking of going back to school for her teaching credential, so that, "I'll be more viable in the world."

13. *Cognitive Behavioral — changing an irrational belief:* Mary, a thirty-eight-year-old teacher, changes an underlying belief that prevents her from taking a better job closer to home. She commutes three hours a day to work with high-risk high school students.

Responsibility. Feeling tremendous responsibility to do the right thing. Do it all, be perfect. They might get struck by lightning or get hit by a train. Overwhelming sense of responsibility. I'm foolish, driven by emotion, rather than being smart or practical. Frustrated. So tired. I'm seeing a big banner that hangs in my classroom: I'm lovable, I'm capable. If I'm not there with that banner, will they be okay? That banner is there for me too.... I'm riding my bike on a road. Feels better. Seeing all the kids' faces. They're okay. Feeling lighter, tension is leaving my body. I'm okay.

When Mary informed her principal about her decision to leave, he offered her a raise. Since she had not yet finished her credential, she decided to stay one more year. She also looked for another teacher to share the commute. She felt that giving herself permission to leave helped her feel better about staying.

❖ *Understanding*

The goal of most therapies includes increased client awareness. Meditative Therapy allows clients to arrive at their own insights. Most therapists acknowledge that an insight which comes from the client is usually more powerful than one coming from the therapist.

1. This client realizes that she is responsible for her part in her problem.

> *What I'm seeing is that I'm not just a victim. I send out vibes too. I tend to think of myself as the center of the universe, but life is much more interactive. It's like bumper cars. We hit each other. I have an impact on people just as they do on me. I need to be aware of that. Whether I don't respond or do so in an unedited fashion, others have to deal with me and it can be overwhelming. It may stimulate emotions and it could be fear. I have an impact on people too.*

2. This female client was tapering off of Xanax. This session listed seven ways to deal with anxiety without using medication.

> *The main thing I'm thinking about — to work on cutting down on my Xanax. It's a lot more than the medicine. It's safety — taking it — knowing I have it. It'll take building up on my strength as a substitute for that — not sure how to do that, although I'm stronger than when I first came in here. What I'd like to know is how to keep building up my strength. One way: to do things I feel afraid of doing. One reason the trip is good for me. It's like building up a muscle — doing it over and over. Another way: realizing that whatever happens is for growth. When I have a panic attack it's showing me an area where I need*

to work on something. A third way: through weakness — let it go. Say, I'll let it go. I have no control. I hope there's a divine order. Let it go. Fourth way: Take care of myself. Do things that are important for myself. Fun. Get new tires. Triple A. Going to seminars. Fifth way: Learning how to communicate — the Giraffe way (assertively). *Sixth: Do my meditation. I should have put that one first. Seventh: Support groups. The Steiner group, church group, coming here. That's it.*

3. This depressed woman arrives at an insight about how her perfectionism is affecting her.

Image of someone hitting me. There's a cushion of space, a buffer zone. He's hitting me fast, but not hurting. I'm not afraid. Even a little bit laughing to myself — seems ridiculous, comical almost. He's starting to get tired. Sitting down with his hands on his head. He's worn out from hitting so much. I'm feeling compassionate. He's the part of me that hits me, gets down on myself. Uses fear to motivate me. I'm feeling more compassion, hearing the words, "You're trying to be perfect."

4. This man was verbally and physically abused as a child. He came in for marital problems due to his temper.

I have an issue with control — like fear of my Dad controlling me. Somewhere along the line I picked up the thought that I would never let anyone else control me.

5. This woman behaved nonassertively with her husband. She frequently gave in to him, then felt resentful later. In this session, she recalled a memory of a camping trip, when he yelled at her for not knowing how to set up the tent.

I had an insight. I need to amplify what I'm feeling, to bring it up. I need to amplify my feelings to figure them out, to see what they are. I was really angry about how D. treated me, but I didn't make a big deal out of it. I just took it, turned the other cheek. No, not really that. Maybe didn't even know what I was feeling. The other morning, I was really feeling it. The time D. didn't go to the picnic. I was really sad. Before I wouldn't have said that, maybe wouldn't have been aware of it. I need to amplify to be aware.

❖ *Reinforcers*

1. This teacher receives a reinforcement for her decision to leave her job and look for a new, less-stressful teaching situation.

> *Picturing myself in a new classroom. They don't have faces. It's okay here. What were you afraid of? Lightness. I'm feeling light. People smiling at me. There's warmth, no tension. I have springy shoes on. I'm springing along. I'm not far from home. Feels really good to me.*

2. At the end of a long abreactive sequence that related to past abuse, this woman felt a sense of freedom.

> *I see beautiful flowers, butterflies, mountains — a beautiful scene. I feel I can breathe. I'm being greeted. Man and woman dressed in robes. Patting me on the back saying, "Job well done." Looking for the young girl. She was laughing. I'm seeing what could have been — self-confidence. She's beautiful. The whole world is in front of her. She can choose.*

3. In this session, a reinforcer helps a client face unpleasant feelings about her husband.

> *Ugly images of my husband, so dark, gloomy, angry. Jekyll-Hyde: happy and laughing; heavy and dark. Turmoil. Trying to stay in there, but I don't want to be there. Oh, an image of angels. Great big wings and white light. Surrounded with their presence. Safety and security. Like I feel I can stay in this much and be okay.*

4. In her first session, this woman resisted the process. She received a feeling of comfort and satisfaction after allowing the process to work.

> *A kind of delight — not sure where it's from. A kind of hope. I thought, "If this is all, it will be interesting." This is a fun game — with the emphasis a child would put on it. With the delight — kind of a good feeling. Beginning to feel very comfortable — almost complacent — an all right-with-the-world feeling. Satisfied.*

❖ *Key Points*

- The two basic goals of Meditative Therapy are the therapeutic goal and the creative goal.

- In achieving the therapeutic goal, the Inner Source process uses six basic methods: discharging, extended discharging, abreaction, treatment, understanding, and reinforcement.

- Examples from case material illustrate a wide variety of individual therapeutic experiences, demonstrating the holistic, individualistic and integrative nature of the Inner Source process.

6 ❖

Creative Experiences in Meditative Therapy

Now, like you, in my reading and in my travels, I had heard about a superior type of man, possessing the keys to everything which is a mystery to us. This idea of a higher and unknown strain within the human race was not something I could take simply as an allegory. Experience has proved, I told myself, that a man cannot reach truth directly nor all by himself. An intermediary has to be present, a force still human in certain respects yet transcending humanity in others. Somewhere on our Earth this superior form of humanity must exist, and not utterly out of our reach. In that case shouldn't all my efforts be directed toward discovering it?

— Rene Daumal

❖   ❖   ❖

As therapists, we understandably focus on the therapeutic quality of any particular therapy. As we have discussed in the previous chapter, the therapeutic quality of the Inner Source — largely concerned with upsetting or traumatic experiences — corresponds to the familiar aspects of most therapies. Although MT offers a new procedure, for the most part, the therapeutic workings are easily identified and understood. The *creative* quality of the Inner Source is equally important, but manifests less frequently, perhaps in ten to fifteen percent of our client population. Creative sequences might be overlooked, because they can be mysterious and are not as widely understood or accepted in the field of psychotherapy.

The complex nature of Meditative Therapy precludes complete understanding of why these creative experiences take place. However, we can speculate about the reasons by observing the effects of creative experiences on clients. In general, creative occurrences seem to stimulate the client's process of awakening, opening up new levels of awareness or new dimensions of being. When this occurs, clients often express amazement and exhilaration. Overall, the creative dimension works toward an expansion of consciousness, and highlights the psycho-spiritual nature of Meditative Therapy. Ancient spiritual traditions and consciousness studies both offer further insight into this aspect of MT. (For further discussion of this topic, see Chapter 13, Roots of Meditative Therapy.)

Three categories of creative experience occur most frequently during MT: unusual light experiences, parapsychological experiences, and new experiences. Although probably not comprehensive, they serve to illustrate this intriguing aspect of the Inner Source process.

Figure 6-1 summarizes the creative experiences in MT. The information presented was derived from content analysis of 423 individual Meditative Therapy sessions, representing 100 clients (54 female, 46 male) who were seen in a university counseling center or in private practice.

Figure 6-1	*Creative Experiences In Meditative Therapy*
Category	**Manifestation**
Unusual Light Experiences	Any type of light Light-dark interaction Bright color Bright light
Parapsychological	**Experiences**

❖ *Unusual Light Experiences*

The experiencing of light has been accorded the highest significance as a spiritual event throughout history. Descriptions of light experiences appear in many spiritual texts, including the *Bible, Bhagavad Gita,* the Egyptian and Tibetan *Books of the Dead,* and *The Secret of the Golden Flower.*

In "Visionary Experience," a lecture given in 1961, Aldous Huxley discusses ancient methods for the induction of visionary experiences. These methods include hypnosis, sensory isolation, one-pointed concentration, breathing, fasting, and the ingestion of mind-altering substances. According to Huxley, the experience of light comprises the greatest common factor of visionary experiences. Light is a major divine symbol. The *Bible* and other religious literature frequently describe the experience of light to signify an encounter with the divine.

Figure 6-2 presents various forms of light experiences reported by a group of 75 clients during MT. 83% of the clients described some form of light experience; 60%, a light-dark interaction; 19%, bright color; 44%, bright light; and 0%, very bright light.

Light experience often occurs with other experiences during MT. It frequently serves to reduce doubt, fear, and resistance to whatever is being presented, and often reinforces belief, joy, peace and resolution.

Unusual light experiences are not a common occurrence in Meditative Therapy, but are always quite meaningful to the client.

Janice's light experience took place in the context of resolution of her infant's death. Eleven years after her baby died, the following sequence occurred after a lengthy abreaction in which she re-experienced the events surrounding his death.

I'm seeing a deep, dark river flowing slowly along. It seems filled with forms of some type. They're bodies. (Deep breath.) All sorts of bodies, young, old, male, female. All nationalities, all those who have ever lived, who have walked the earth. They've worked, loved, lived and died. So many, just flowing along. The river comes to a cliff and a falls. At the point of the falls, sparks of light emanate from each body. The sparks expand outward into an intense bright light. I'm seeing this happening over and over. A sense of release and even joy. This is the process. My son is there in the light, a radiant, blissful feeling.

Figure 6-2		*Manifestation of Various Types of Light Experience Occurring in a Group of 75 Counseling Clients*

Experience	Percent Reporting	Typical Examples
Any type of light	83%	"I keep getting flashes, like sheet lightning." "My eyes have a very light stroboscopic effect, a light blinking, only on the left side, though." "Like light radiating from concentric circles." "Picture the sun, feel the warmth of the sun." "All of a sudden it seems light in here (opens and closes eyes). I don't know if that was the cue (to finish the session) or not. Did you turn the light on? ('No') Oh."
Light-dark interaction	60%	"There is a dark tunnel with faint light at the end." "Darkness and a few light spots in my visual field, kind of a sweeping motion to the right, like a windshield wiper wiping away. It got lighter." "Light and dark that swirls around like clouds, reminds me of Greek mythology – in the beginning there was chaos." "Almost like an entrance to a cave, there's a darkness and a lightness." "Something about dark and light. Darkness negative and evil, light is like good stuff. I'm wandering around in my mind between them."
Bright color	19%	"Very bright red on the left." "A lot of bright blue light." "Bright-colored foil."
Bright light	44%	"Like I'm waking up, real bright, like looking at the sun with eyes closed." "Feel like it's got a bright light on in there." "Hmmm, a real bright flash will come. So bright. If you were looking, you would want to turn your head."

After the session she commented, "I'm really amazed this came up. I've dealt with it in so many other ways, therapy, journaling — you name it, I've done it. Experiencing the light sparks completes it now. I have a strong sense of knowing that the soul continues on and that the body is just a form. It's a peaceful feeling."

The expression, "the light of understanding," is also apparent in the following twenty-minute excerpt from Pam's MT session. She initiated therapy to deal with resentment towards her husband. She had just filed for divorce and no longer had contact with her husband, but was "haunted" by eleven years of mistreatment. He had multiple extra-marital affairs during their marriage and had pressured her to get an abortion, against her will.

(9:15 a.m.) *I get the feeling that I'm going to have to go on with my life. I'm going to have to start my life. I just see these two hands behind me pushing me. I'm kind of bending at the middle, like a resistance thing. Now I see two praying hands* (stomach gurgles). *I can't understand why I don't trust my husband and I just saw that brick wall and door again* (starts sobbing). *It seems that if I'd ever get through that door somehow I'd trust or feel good, but I don't know how to get through the door. It's like I'm sitting on one side and trying to figure out how to get through it. I just got a flash. Why don't you just open it? Why try and scheme and connive to get what you want? Why not just go the direct way? Something is holding me back from opening the door or I don't know how to go the direct way. Something's holding me back.* (9:30 a.m.) (Deep breath.) *My body is going back and forth and all of a sudden I think this is ridiculous. I'll either stay and open it or walk away. I know why I'm afraid, it's because there's not going to be anything on the other side* (deep breath). *I don't remember opening it, but I'm looking on the other side. There is a light there, like a big expanse of nothing, but it's white. And clear, and a bright light there that's giving me light to work with. And a pen is writing on it. I just saw the word "respect," but it's not written on that table. The ones on the table are written, but there are no words. I just saw the word "word" and I can see a little figure of a person on this great big white sheet, and it's walking toward these squiggle lines.* (9:35 a.m.)

In her follow-up inventory, Jennifer reported that, "I am no longer hurt by events that took place. I have also completely released my former husband emotionally. I have gained a great deal of inner strength in knowing I can positively handle events in my life. Meditative Therapy was a beautiful experience for me. It has given me a tremendous sense of inner peace." Jennifer's sense of healing and strength seemed related to her light experience that highlighted the importance of respect.

David, a twenty-two-year-old college student, came to therapy to increase his self-confidence and reduce his anxiety. He experienced anxiety over sexual performance and his recent engagement. He was afraid of being rejected and of failing. Physical symptoms such as nail biting, stomach trouble, bowel disturbances, and headaches bothered him. He described his goal as follows: "I have a great many diversified talents, which I need to coalesce as a whole unit, me." In the following excerpt from his fourth MT session, David experienced three different metaphoric sequences of death and rebirth.

(1:30 p.m.) *That area* (described before) *where it felt like I had pain in my back became a white line. Like I could see it became a white line and it bulged at the top and became a big bulge, and then it started to bulge at the bottom and formed into a, still a white line in a black background and then it formed these two bulges. Then it flashed over to a color, kind of, and it was a fetus still in the sack, still kind of floating, and it was looking at me with really black eyes. The whole thing was solid black, the eyes were. There was not white around the eyes, or anything.*

And it sounded like the voice of a really old, old man, and it was talking to me. And it said, "A whole powered man," as if it was asking a question, and it sounded like there was a choir that said, "It is good, it is good." Thousands of voices. Then it said, "A whole is a composite part of a unit," and the choir would sing, "It is good, it is good," again. Then finally it said, "Unite the being and you unite the verses," and it went, "It is good, it is good," and then there was this big flash of white light out of the right side across my visual field. The visual field turned really a soft cream color and then I saw a gun, the barrel of a gun sticking out, kind of looking at an angle down the barrel, and I saw a flash of yellow and I could kind of see the burning grains of gun powder and saw the bullet slowly moving out the end; it's really, really slow. And it hit somebody's forehead and it went in and kind of pushed its way in and the skin closed over behind it, and then the side of the head was completely cut open and I could, it looks like I was looking at a bunch of people, and as the bullet went through, it was tearing them all apart and a lot screams from all these people getting torn apart. And it worked its way towards the back of the head, the back of the head just exploded and all these bodies, these little tiny human bodies were all blowing around, and just shooting up and down. Hmm. (Pause.)

The head seemed to close back, the pieces came back toward the back of the head and fused over, kind of closed over. And the people remaining in the head kind of rearranged themselves into a huge kind of sphere of people. They are all sitting around in a circle, a concentric circle, but all around the inside of the head. Right in the absolute center there is a bright glow and all the people started clapping. I felt like I was at the top of the head looking down and all the people in the head were clapping, women and men together in there, all naked sitting around in there, and they started chanting, "en cha, en cha." It looked like a woman at first was all of a sudden spinning by this fire, like all I could see was long black hair spinning around, and when it stopped, it was short and all I could see was two large eyes from behind the hair, and the chanting was still going on and all the clapping and everybody reached out and seemed to fuse together and the glow in the middle started to go out through everybody. Then the whole inside of the head was glowing; then all of a sudden it was just snuffed out. I realized that the person, whoever it was that got shot, was dead (short silence).

I was kneeling down and had my head on a block and had my head chopped off, and I picked up my head, put it in my arm, and was standing up and it was on a platform in front of a large crowd of people. It was spraying blood out of my neck, like a fountain at everybody, and I said, 'Come all ye people, gather round,' and my head down here was smiling. The blood would hit the people and hit them right on the chest right above the heart and then they would start smiling, and then he said something about coming to the end of the time, and so I felt I was sitting on this bluff above the sea looking out over the ocean and it looked like just the end of the sunset where the sky is getting really dark and still a few streaks of light, the clouds way out there, and I felt like I could see it with the head that was on my shoulders and I reached up and I couldn't see and it felt like I was looking in the mirror, couldn't see the head, but I knew there was one up there. So I took the one that was under my arm and threw it out in the ocean. Soon as it hit the water, it started rising and all these clouds started getting lighter and lighter and it was just a big sun up in the air. (2:05 p.m.)

At first, this excerpt might seem unusual and mysterious. Remember from the previous chapter, that the Inner Source frequently speaks through metaphor. These three sequences combine an extended, complex metaphor with light imagery. The white light, the bright glow and the light of the sun add power to the metaphoric death of the fragmented self and rebirth of a unified self.

The first sequence of the fetus introduces the theme of wholeness or unity, "a whole powered man." The chorus amplifies the message, "Unite the being and you unite the verse." The second sequence achieves new unity through a symbolic death by shooting. The death of the disorganized or fragmented personality is represented by the blowing apart of the tiny human beings inside the head. A rebirth occurs when the beings form a circle and chant together, representing unity.

In the third sequence, David witnesses his death by decapitation, which emphasizes the rebirth theme through repetition. Ironically, this death allows David to relate more lovingly to others, for it is the blood of suffering which strikes their hearts and brings smiles. In the final striking image, the old head when cast out into the ocean, becomes a sun, a symbol for the expanded or true self.

Shortly after this last sequence the session ended. He had one more session, which followed the same metaphorical approach by the Inner Source. He enjoyed all of the sessions and stated that his mind became more peaceful and less concerned about the things in life which he could do nothing about. His anxiety diminished and his self-confidence increased. He also reported feeling more whole, saying, "I realize now that my mind and body are connected. They're not separate."

These three different client sessions all involved experiencing unusual light sequences. All three clients reported that the light made an impact on them. It seemed to increase the power of whatever material was being presented. All three clients improved significantly after their light experiences. Carl Jung, in his commentary on *The Secret of the Golden Flower,* Wilhelm (1962), acknowledged the therapeutic and creative effects of the vision of light. He stated that:

> *Its effect is astonishing in that it almost always brings about a solution of psychic complications, and thereby frees the inner personality from emotional and intellectual entanglements, creating thus a unity of being which is universally felt as "liberation."*

❖ *Parapsychological Experiences*

A variety of experiences occur during Meditative Therapy that defy ordinary, logical explanation. Parapsychological or psychic events (We use these terms interchangeably) transcend our perception of reality through the known five senses. J. B. Rhine and J. Pratt (1957), in *Parapsychology, The Frontier Science of the Mind,* define parapsychology as "a division of psychology dealing with behavioral or personal effects that are demonstrably nonphysical (that is, which do not fall within the scope of physical principles)."

The following excerpts from MT sessions illustrate the ability of the Inner Source to generate parapsychological experiences. In general, these experiences tend to widen clients' awareness of the nature of reality. They also often increase the client's sense of oneness with God. Parapsychological events include precognition, past lives experiences, communication with discarnate entities, and out-of-body experiences.

Precognition (Prior knowledge of an event). An hour after his first Meditative Therapy session, Jim, a twenty-five-year-old college student, attended a movie. During the movie, an actor repeated the same phrase that he had heard earlier in his MT session. Jim's precognitive experience impacted him dramatically. "Hearing the words in that way really got my attention. I realized that I needed to make a change. It made my Meditative Therapy session more powerful. It was a wake-up call," Jim stated.

Stephen, a thirty-eight-year-old minister, came into therapy to deal with a recent separation from his wife. She had filed for divorce, but he still loved her and wanted to work on the relationship. She refused all attempts at reconciliation. His MT session foreshadowed their reunion.

> *I'm traveling on a train. Walking down the aisle, feeling the back and forth motion of the train. I see a woman with dark hair, holding a baby, at the end of the car. As I approach her, I realize that she is my wife. The baby turns his head and smiles. He has deep blue eyes. I know that he is my son.*

Stephen reacted to this precognition by feeling assured that the marriage would work out. He decided to give his wife time and wait and see. His precognition was confirmed two years later, when Stephen's wife decided to return to the marriage.

Past Lives Experiences (Previous lives in past historical periods). During MT, clients frequently experience seeing themselves in other historical periods. The following excerpts occurred without prompting clients that past life experiences might happen. It is impossible to determine the veracity of these reports as authentic past-life material. Perhaps they were "made up" from books or movies or occur as metaphoric representations of current issues. However, the clients who experienced these sequences accepted them as real and reported significant changes after these sessions.

Betty, a twenty-eight-year-old nurse, suffered from recurrent depression and irritability. She experienced the following past life sequence:

> *A mother and child are walking by a palomino horse, playing with a wagon in the back. Going across the prairies, sort of see mountain range, trees to the right. A long way to go, walking, dusty, have thick heavy coats on, maybe it's cold. I'm getting a headache.*
>
> *Now it's sort of like split vision, now a wagon train on the right side and something above similar to the Parthenon, but new. No connection between the two, not even the same country. Now more animals with the wagon train, a lot of cows. Kind of seems to be taking over on the bottom. Top could have been a monastery.*
>
> *A little girl with the woman instead of a boy. Not a palomino horse anymore. No men, just women and children, dust, dry. I don't feel like crying, but I'm starting to tear up (sobbing). Oh, it's dry. I'm so tired. I just want to go, oh, oh*

(crying). *It's all dark now, just like night, seems like I can still hear the cows. I see the outline of the wagon and firelight. It's cold,* (breathes deeply) *feels like I am sleeping under the wagon. Still see women out there cleaning. Hear men laughing and talking. See an older woman now, twenty or twenty-two, wearing a shawl. I feel warm; bed I'm in feels like another body close to me. See her with long skirts swishing around, talking to me a little bit. Some soldiers riding up, quite a few, circling the camp, wagons too. Gee, looks like there are many of them. I'm getting scared. Girl comes back to the wagon. She is comforting the little girl. Doesn't feel like me. Man on horse talking. Everyone starts getting ready. We're supposed to go with them, don't know why* (crying). *I don't know what's happening. We're following, don't know where we are going. Oh, uh.* (Breathing heavily.) *All I can see is blue night. No one's talking. Everyone's quiet. I don't even think they are taking the cows.*

See some men throwing spears on top of our wagons, killing our horses (sobbing). *How did they get there? Fire. Oh, it's on fire. I can't get out! One next to me on fire, can't get out! Uh, oh, oh,* (sobbing). *I feel like I'm being stampeded by horses and wagons. Oh, uh, someone is bending over me, like soldiers putting a blanket over me. Dead. Oh, feels like a relief, oh, uh, oh. I see soldiers and wagon, charred, not burnt to the ground.*

Woman's dead. He's laying her next to me, covering her with a blanket too. Digging some holes, only two soldiers. Where are other people? Put us in some grave, others on top of us, two others, three. Covered with dirt. Riding away. See lots of dead horses, burnt out wagons. Everybody's dead (takes several breaths).

After this session, Betty reported an elevation of mood and less irritability. She stated, "I feel good about me now. I haven't felt that way for a long time. Feels like I was cleaned out inside. I'm having a lot of positive things going through my mind now." At a three-month follow-up phone call, she stated, "An inner sense of tranquility has persisted since my last counseling experience. I still get angry and tired, but this seems to be on the surface. There is an inner quietness now." Eighteen months later, Betty reported that this feeling of inner quietness and tranquillity remained.

Communication with Discarnate Entities (Communicating
with the spirits of the dead). Interest in the United States on
communication with discarnate entities has been stimulated by
the works of Elizabeth Kubler-Ross (1975) on death and dying,
and Raymond Moody (1975) on near-death experiences. Karlis
Osis, Ph.D., collected significant information on this subject as
early as 1960 in a work called *Deathbed Observations by Physicians
and Nurses.* In Meditative Therapy, this type of creative
experience usually helps clients process unresolved grief issues.

Margaret, forty-two, experienced multiple deaths in her
childhood and adolescence. Her mother and sister were killed in
an auto accident when she was eighteen months old. Her
grandmother raised her, but was killed in a car accident when
Margaret was seventeen. Margaret's neck was broken in this
collision and several vertebrae were injured. Her father, an
alcoholic, died a year later. Margaret suffered from dysthymia,
depression, anxiety, and problems with relationships. She also
feared that she would some day die in an auto accident.

*The light is walking with me, has my hand, but I don't have
one. I don't understand much of what is happening. There are a
whole bunch of dead faces, past faces, not skeletons, just past
dead faces. There is a diamond, a diamond star sapphire with
all the projections gleaming out in all directions. There is an
opening right through and it's as if I'm looking through it.*

*I see through to eternity. Oh, absolutely beautiful. I have
chills all over, almost too beautiful* (voice cracks). *A great big
flower just turned up. Not a lot of color, purple. Somebody in
the middle of it. Like it is me when I was a happy child, a happy
child. I don't remember. Definitely a happy child. A coffin*
(starts sobbing). *My mother, they won't let me see her. Mommy,
oh Mommy* (sobbing). *She's in the box. Oh, Mommy! The box
broke up into all kinds of cubicles, different shapes.*

The light is still around (sobbing stops). *I don't want to
leave my mother, but the light says we have to go. I have one
hand reached back. I don't want to move away. I can see my
mother's face. I don't remember seeing her face before, other
than in pictures. Incredibly sweet, smiling, holds her hand out
and says it's okay to go* (sobbing). *I feel like I've never touched
her. I hold her hand just for one minute more. Oh, it would have*

been so nice to have you around, Mom. It's been lonely without you! She still says it is okay to go. She's okay (deep breath). *A big sunburst again* (coughs). *I'm really in a cold sweat, uh, uh, clogged up. It is light like at home, but it's not that light in here, no windows here. I still want to stay with mother, but her face is going out to the side of the picture. She says she'll be there though. Gone now* (deep breaths, sobbing).

There's still a shadow of light where she left me. A lot darker in the sky now, more stars, but still darker (deep breath). *I'm having trouble giving up the coffin; I want to hold on to it* (deep breath). *I see a picture of me taken sitting on the grass by mother's grave. I know now why I looked the way I did. I must have understood a lot about it. I must have been three then, I couldn't have been eighteen months. An eighty-year-old, three-year-old. Black water on a white beach, waves roll up and mix. I'm really dry, have trouble breathing. Body is not as tight as usual.*

Now I see a movie theater screen. Black heads watching a white screen. I'm looking at people from the front now. All people that are dead. Grandmother (starts sobbing), *us, I miss you! She says I'm doing fine, she's really pleased. She's sorry she had to go, she wanted to stay too. I want to put my head on her knee* (deep breath). *The light is very much around. Behind my grandmother. She's not smiling, but she looks peaceful. She's happy. Like I'm having a conversation with her, but she's not moving her mouth. I just hear it. Says she's not in pain anymore. She says I'm having some of my pain for her and I don't need to. Weird, she says she can rock as long as she wants to rock. The light is moving on, says we've got to go* (sobbing, choking sounds).

I see the sunburst again. My sister. I don't know her except from pictures, but she's grown up, not three, looks like three, but, I don't understand. She's very beautiful (sobbing). *Oh, oh. She wants to know me too, but we'll never have that chance. Maybe some day. She seems like a wise, old woman. It's the eyes. It's just her head. I don't see her body. The light is very much right there too. Very beautiful. The light says we have to go.*

A voice says I can let go with my hand from the light, that I don't need to hang on to it, it will still be there. I feel like I'm waiting for a rainbow, all movement is going in that direction, but I don't see one. Sunrise, bright sun, no color, rainbow out in the middle of the sunrise. It is faint and little, all the way up to the top (deep breath, opens eyes).

Margaret received much comfort and support from this creative experience. At the end of this session, she commented "That was the first contact with my mother. I'm afraid to ask if it is possible to talk to those people, but I sure heard them." In the following weeks, she reported having fewer "nightmare-filled nights " and feeling "more buoyant" and "definitely not alone — connected to God and also my mom, Sis and Grandmother."

Out-of-Body Experiences (OOB's) (The soul leaves the physical body and travels). It is very difficult to verify out of body experiences, but Dr. Charles Tart, a psychologist at the University of California at Davis, has made significant scientific inroads into the matter. One of Tart's OOB subjects could read a randomly selected five-digit number placed on a shelf far above her bed. Her spirit body, while traveling out of her physical body, could locate and correctly report the number. (Tart, 1990)

The OOB experience is the most commonly occurring parapsychological event of Meditative Therapy. The experience varies in length from a few minutes to longer segments of twenty to sixty minutes. For most clients, this is the first OOB experience of their lives. Some individuals will leave their bodies between sessions, but this is rare. Most clients respond to this creative experience by feeling a stronger spiritual connection. This enhances their ability to put their problems into perspective and often stimulates new solutions. One client said that her MT out-of-body experience "increased my awareness of myself as almost independent of myself — an appraising."

Ben, a thirty-two-year-old college professor, described the following OOB experience in his sixth session of Meditative Therapy. After a divorce and a failure to receive a promotion, he felt depressed and lacked self-confidence. He expressed this negative view of himself as, "I just can't do anything right."

(1:58 p.m.) *I'm beginning to feel myself sort of drop into a deeper sense of relaxation — a feeling of letting go, almost like falling. That feels very good just to let everything go. I notice that my breathing is very weak or shallow, but I don't need much any more. Very good feeling just to breathe very little. I can't even feel my heart beating* (seven-minute silence — outwardly, it appeared as if he might have fallen asleep).

I feel like I'm sort of detached. For a short time I didn't have any real sense of where I was or what time it was. I saw a fish, very large, sort of lying on its side. It was on the beach, a pleasant feeling about it. I saw a very docile black-and-white dog. Very large dog with a thin face like an Afghan. A calm, very friendly dog, not asleep, but resting. Then I got such a feeling of being detached, like I could go anywhere I wanted to go — sort of leave my body behind, just because I wanted to, and free myself of all physical limits and just be anywhere I wanted to be. And I sort of went somewhere — not sure where I went. I couldn't tell you how long. No sense of time or physical place. Just before that I was very aware of my breathing in that I couldn't feel myself breathing. Not sure that I was breathing. When I came back from wherever I went I was a little startled and a little disappointed to come back. (2:16 p.m.)

I feel so good about it that I would like to go back again. It's sort of like tapping a new resource that I've known was there for a long time, but I was kind of out of touch with. Now the fingers in my hands and the back of my neck feel very thick. It's a good feeling. Now my eyelids feel that way. Now it feels a little uncomfortable, like a, like the need to move (opens eyes, moves hands and feet). *I guess that's it.* (2:25 p.m.)

Whether or not Ben actually had an OOB experience, he reported feeling empowered by his session. He described its effect on him as follows: "That feeling of being able to just transcend the physical and go anywhere I want to was really an exhilarating feeling. And it wasn't like dreaming; it was a real feeling. But it was sort of like I just tapped into it, discovered it, but didn't really use it." When he returned one week later he stated that he had thought about the experience all week long. He attributed his new sense of self-confidence in his capabilities to this MT experience.

❖ *New Experiences*

New experiences include unusual sensations or experiences outside of the normal parameter of everyday experiences; a felt sense of physical motion (spinning, floating, rocking, and vibrating), changes in body size or shape, alterations in body temperature, and time distortions. Here are a few client descriptions of this type of experience:

> *I'm spinning…Oh, I'm in a centrifuge. Oh, I'm trying to open my eyes and I can't. I can't stop it. It's fast, faster. Why am I spinning so fast? It's kind of scaring me, it's going so fast.*

> *It feels like in an airplane, banking. I am. I'm actually banking, moving very fast. Space program, strapped, moving in a circle. Fast. Dizzy, like I'm drunk.*

> *I see black waves. Feels like I'm falling down a hole.*

> *I can't really see or feel anything. Void. Total darkness. No time or space, just endless. I thought my heart stopped for a second, I couldn't even feel it.*

> *Picturing a white mass, but no distinct mass to it. Not like a sphere, but spherical. White streaks coming off of it at the center, but not a distinct center. Energy, like the state of Transcendental Meditation. Makes my head feel different. Tension in my forehead rises and gets lighter and lighter. I get to the point of kind of floating around.*

> *I feel so cold. I know it's warm in here, but I'm freezing. Feels like a cold winter wind.*

> *I'm shaking apart! No, it's uh, oh, oh, oh* (arms are shaking). *Like I'm rocking back and forth, rocking, vibrating. A big empty space like I was breaking into thousands of pieces. Oh, oh, gosh. I feel like I've landed like a leaf when it falls to the ground. It kind of floats. Oh, it feels good. My body feels the way it should feel, not floating. Feels very, very solid, not like I'm going to fall apart again — never.*

> *Feels like my whole left side is growing, stretching longer than my right side. I really feel uneven. Am I uneven? Wow,*

it's very real. My left leg feels about two feet longer than my right leg.

My back feels rounded, hard, curled up like a beetle. I'm a beetle. Rocking back and forth on my back. I feel very small. Powerless.

I feel like someone is blowing me up again and I fill out the shape I'm supposed to be. I feel like some big speed is going to overtake me and I have to protect myself in a ball, and it goes faster and faster and now one from behind swirling up and it's spinning and spinning...like I'm being sucked up into a whirlpool, but faster. This is happening all over my left side. Makes me have to breathe shorter...I'm swinging over to the left, but I'm not trying to. Because the left side of my neck is tired from pulling, but I'm pulling back and it is all clear. My body just rolls around. I have to hold my arms straight by my sides and tuck my chin in and I'm rolling around and also pivoting in a circle, like spokes on a wheel. I guess it slowed down. I can take deeper breaths. That's a relief. And my head is turned back over to straight. I almost feel like I'm panting.

Clients feel these types of experiences intensely. For example, the woman who felt cold habitually brought a wool coat to wear during Meditative Therapy. In spite of this, feeling cold continued for several sessions. Often clients ask if their body has changed size or shape. Clients' reactions to having such unusual sensations vary. Responses include amazement, fear, exhilaration, exhaustion, relief and curiosity about why such experiences occur.

We can only speculate about why the Inner Source generates these types of creative experiences. Some of these experiences may be discharges from somatic sensations linked to past experiences such as pain or fevers from illnesses and dizziness or nausea from carnival rides. Others seem to offer symbolic experiences aimed at intensifying an issue or feeling. For example, the client, who became small and beetle-like, dramatically experienced her feelings of being powerless, unable to make decisions, and move forward in life. She reacted against this repugnant sensation by taking charge of her circumstances. Finally, some creative experiences such as whirling and feeling light may foster a spiritual awakening. These experiences resemble various spiritual practices such as dancing, whirling, or meditating.

It is important to discuss these experiences after the Meditative Therapy session to help clients process them and arrive at their own meanings of their unusual experience.

❖ *Key Points*

- Creative experiences appear to stimulate the client's spiritual awakening, that is, the process of opening up to new levels of awareness or the expansion of consciousness.

- Creative sequences usually present experiences outside of normal, physical reality such as unusual light experiences, parapsychological experiences, and new experiences.

- Creative experiences are often intensely felt and can create profound effects that may need to be processed at the end of the session.

7 ❖

Helping Clients with Fears and Resistance

I feel cold and clammy now, but I still feel like I'm fighting, half of me wants to go on, half doesn't. I'm not seeing anything. It is really dark, cavernous and underground. I had a lot of sleep last night. I'm not tired, but it is just like having a sheet dropped over me. Maybe I can go someplace where I don't know where I am. I feel pressure in my chest. My neck is still hurting an awful lot. Really strange because I don't feel that much pain usually. I'm looking for an answer to why I can't remember what happened. My face feels tight again. I want to get up. I'm just terrified. I'm terrified and I don't even know why. I feel like I'm tightening all over just to keep things out or in or something.

The above client excerpt illustrates resistance to the process of MT. When fears become stimulated, clients often express an ambivalence about continuing or even a desire to stop. Most resistance in Meditative Therapy is based on fears of various kinds; clients don't cooperate when they are afraid. Clinicians must anticipate such reactions and prepare clients by exploring each client's concerns or fears surrounding the process prior to MT, educating clients about these fears, supporting clients during MT when they become afraid, and debriefing any fears after an MT session.

Clients frequently express six major fears regarding Meditative Therapy: (1) fear of self-disclosure, (2) fear of deep mental illness, (3) fear of pain and discomfort, (4) fear of losing control, (5) fear of failure and (6) fear that the therapy is not working properly. We'll examine each of these fears in this chapter.

75

❖ Fear of Self-Disclosure

Sometimes due to embarrassment, shame, or the desire to protect the therapist, the client does not want to share with the therapist what he or she experiences during MT. Since the client's continual verbalization is an important aspect of MT, this fear must be addressed. In order to assess this fear, the therapist might ask, "Is there anything that might come up in our sessions that you might have difficulty sharing?" If the client answers affirmatively, the therapist can explore this further: "What has happened that might be hard for you to talk about?" "What makes it difficult for you to talk about this?"

Therapists can use this opportunity to normalize the client's feelings of embarrassment or shame. For example, Mary felt ashamed to talk about a molestation that occurred when she was seven. When reassured that many victims feel ashamed, even though the shame belongs to the adult perpetrator, Mary was able to explore this feeling. She related that she hadn't stopped her uncle and wondered if this meant that she was responsible. After talking about the incident, Mary realized that as a seven-year-old, it wasn't her responsibility to stop her uncle.

When this fear occurs during a session, clients may give general or minimal reports. For example, Dave's report became hesitant and vague, as he struggled with shame over several date rapes. "Em...well, just some old memories...scenes from a party when I was in college." When the therapist asked him to report exactly what he was seeing, he became silent. The therapist then asked what kept him from saying what was happening. He proceeded to explain his fears that he would be rejected by the therapist and possibly even turned over to the police. After he explored his fears and felt reassured that he could talk about what happened in a safe, non-judgmental context, he was able to continue the session. In such cases, even though the limits of confidentiality have been discussed, the reporting laws should be clarified, as they pertain to the client's situation.

Clients who have witnessed atrocities may be reluctant to describe such events for fear of traumatizing the therapist. In such cases, the clients should be reassured that the therapist can handle hearing about such events and that it's important to describe them. For example, a Vietnam veteran witnessed the torture death of a fellow soldier. The soldier had been staked out and then skinned alive. When he came to this memory, he said, "I don't know if you would want to hear this…. It's pretty bad. No one should have to hear about this…. It's bad enough just thinking about it…." In this case, the therapist encouraged him to trust what was coming up and to continue reporting what he was seeing. The therapist reassured him by saying, "It's okay to tell me, I can handle it. It's important for you to work through this. Just stay with it and continue to tell me what you're getting." This allowed the client to continue. After a short description of the incident, the focus shifted to the client's feelings of helplessness and anger over not being able to rescue the soldier.

After the session, the therapist can follow up by exploring the client's reaction to having disclosed embarrassing, shameful or horrific events. Added support for having talked about uncomfortable sequences can help clients feel better about such disclosures. Pointing out their courage in proceeding can enhance their self-esteem. This is also an opportune time to underscore the importance of trusting the Inner Source, facing the discomfort, and working through disturbing memories and feelings.

❖ *Fear of Deep Mental Illness*

The very setting of Meditative Therapy provokes fears in a certain percentage of clients. Lying down on a couch seems to stimulate fears of going to a "shrink," being analyzed, or being identified as "crazy." In addition, closing the eyes may bring up fears of uncovering a deep dark secret which cannot be faced. Once again, sharing and exploring these fears with the therapist often frees the client to proceed.

For example, Betty, a twenty-three-year-old university student, explained that she was afraid of going crazy, if she faced feelings surrounding her sister's suicide. She had become manic after the death of her sister, ten years earlier. When this fear was further explored, Betty revealed that the family refused to talk about these events and took a long vacation in order to forget about what happened. The emotional distress of suppressing her feelings had apparently triggered Betty's manic episode. The therapist reassured Betty that talking about her feelings and working through her anger and grief would most likely benefit rather than harm her.

Sometimes the client fears the unknown. For example, Mark was afraid of discovering something "horrible." He compared his fear to standing in front of a locked closet door and not knowing what he would find if he opened it. The thirty-eight-year-old city planner worried that he might discover something bad about himself or another family member. When asked what something bad might be, he talked about his father's history of bipolar disorder. He also had heard of people finding out in therapy that they had been sexually abused as children by a family member. Perhaps he would discover that he also had been molested and that's why he was "so screwed up" now. Mark's fear seemed to concern being damaged by mental illness, as he believed his father had been. The therapist then prepared Mark to deal with sequences that might concern his father's illness and his concerns about his own mental health. Mark needed encouragement to face these unpleasant feelings. In addition, the therapist addressed Mark's fear regarding repressed memories.

The topic of retrieval of repressed memories may need to be dealt with in order for some clients to proceed. The retrieval of a memory of a molestation during MT, when absolutely no previous memory exists, is unlikely. Any such occurrences should be treated very carefully and clients should be educated about the possible confusion or misinterpretation surrounding such memories.

During MT, clients may re-experience memories that suggest some sort of abuse. However, it's not always possible to ascertain the veracity of the actual experience versus the memory of this experience. Since these memories come from a child's viewpoint, it's often difficult to know exactly what happened without some outer verification. For example, during MT, Sarah saw herself as a five-year-old, sitting on the toilet. She felt afraid when she saw blood in the toilet. From this short segment, she wondered if she had been molested. When asked what other possible explanations might exist for the blood, she considered that it might have been her mother's menstrual blood or blood from a urinary tract infection or kidney injury. She decided to check this memory out with her family. Since her mother was dead and her father or sisters didn't remember the incident, she never figured out what had happened. However, further MT sessions did not develop the theme of molestation. Future sessions focused on her exceptional sensitivity as a child and her feelings of alienation from other family members, who ridiculed her for this quality.

Of course, it could have turned out that Sarah had been molested. If this were the case, it is likely that subsequent sessions would have developed along this line. Even in this case, the identity of the perpetrator or the details may remain hidden. In these cases, it's best for both therapist and client not to draw premature conclusions, but to allow the therapy to express whatever issues need to be resolved.

❖ *Fear of Pain and Discomfort*

Prior to MT, the therapist should explain that both positive and negative events may take place during Meditative Therapy. Such experiences of emotional discomfort as crying and feeling physical aches or pains occur frequently. When clients understand the therapeutic value of staying with uncomfortable experiences, they usually can allow the MT process to proceed. Pointing out that whatever we don't talk about or face "runs the show," usually makes sense to the client. Becoming aware that their symptoms or difficulties arise from efforts to avoid disturbing issues often motivates clients to deal with these issues.

In particular, clients with a history of trauma should understand that an abreaction, the re-experiencing of a traumatic event, may occur. Preparing clients for this eventuality makes such an occurrence less frightening. An abreaction is an intense physical, psychological, and/or spiritual experience which focuses on an event or cluster of events centering around a past traumatic experience. Such experiences may involve the fear of death or loss. These events include: *natural disasters,* such as floods, earthquakes and fires; *accidents,* like auto collisions, home fires, or severe falls; *abuse,* such as physical, emotional, or sexual abuse; *war experiences;* and *death and near-death experiences* due to serious illness or accidents.

Usually abreactions appear dramatic and are accompanied by violent physical reactions such as writhing, sobbing, yelling, shaking and intense feelings like anger, shame, grief or guilt. Other abreactions may be "quietly intense." The client may experience the intensity inwardly without much outward expression. The intensity may range from the same level of disturbance experienced during the original occurrence to substantially lower levels. Clients may re-experience whatever sensations, emotions, and thoughts were present during the original experience.

Prior to MT, the therapist should reassure the client that abreactions are normal and therapeutic, even though they may be disturbing or painful. Most clients describe the upset and pain as beneficial, once they are through it, because of the resulting lessening of stress and disturbance surrounding the traumatic events. Many MT sessions that include abreaction are followed by a dramatic reduction in the client's symptoms. Clients should be encouraged to stay with an abreaction until it concludes. This allows the emotional intensity to discharge and resolve naturally. When clients understand the importance of staying with an abreaction, they are more likely to continue if one occurs in later sessions. Clients must also be given permission to stop if necessary. It is always the client's choice whether or not to continue.

The following client statements reflect the high levels of disturbance that can accompany an abreaction: "Oh God, I'm in that doctor's office!" "I hate them! I hate them!" "I'm so ashamed!" "This is the worst experience I've ever been through!" The therapist must be comfortable with such intense sequences and remain calm and supportive during the abreaction. Such an atmosphere creates a sense of safety for the client. Encouraging statements from the therapist help clients stay with the experience. Encouragers such as "That's good. Just stay with it," "You're doing great. You can get through it," "You're safe here. It's safe to see this now," convey the therapist's calm, supportive presence to the client. Such statements also remind clients that they will make it through the experience. In this manner, the therapist reinforces the value of undergoing the experience.

Clients also need to be given permission to stop if the abreaction becomes overwhelming. Sometimes a short break and discussion of what is happening can help a client feel safe enough to continue. For example, Gina experienced intense shaking accompanied by nausea. She was very worried about the possibility of vomiting in the office. She stopped and shared this fear. The therapist provided a wastebasket and reassured her that it was okay to throw up. This allowed Gina to continue and after five minutes, the nausea resolved. However, in some cases, clients might actually vomit. A short break can allow clients to remember that they are in the therapist's office, that the therapist supports them, that they are in charge and can ask for what they need, and that they'll feel better once they get through the abreaction.

If the client chooses to stop in the middle of an abreaction and not continue, closure should be achieved by exploring the client's reaction to the session and by using a closure exercise. (See appendix G.) For example, Claudia stopped in the middle of an abreaction dealing with being drowned as a seven-year-old by her mother, who was schizophrenic. She explained that she felt scared that her mother was actually in the office and would harm her for telling. She knew this was not a rational belief, but as a child had believed that her mother possessed magical powers. When asked what she needed to feel safe, she said she needed to go to her safe place. Prior to beginning MT, Claudia had created a safe place, a garden scene at her aunt's house. Now she could visualize her safe place, and the overwhelming feelings of fear diminished. Two days later, she reported that she had felt that overwhelming fear again. While she was driving, she felt that her mother was in the car with her and was trying to force her off the road. This thought triggered a panic attack. This experience helped her realize the need to face her fear. She was able to return to MT and stay with the abreaction until it resolved. This session marked a turning point in Claudia's feeling safer and more in control of her own life. Her panic attacks decreased both in frequency and severity.

When a client elects to stop, acknowledging the client's feelings in a supportive, non-judgmental manner avoids the implication that the client has failed or lacks courage, etc. In such cases, other therapies can help clients process feelings regarding their issues. Sand Play therapy, talk therapy, or art therapy may feel like safer alternatives to the client. These methods may pave the way for later use of Meditative Therapy.

At the end of any session which contains an abreaction, the therapist should help the client process any feelings or thoughts related to the abreaction. This helps clients express both positive and negative reactions. The therapist should listen for any negative self-statements centering around guilt, shame, or blame and help clients explore these feelings.

The following response illustrates Liz's reaction to an abreaction concerning her mother's suicide attempt.

I remembered you warning me that I might have an intense reaction during MT, but hearing about that is different than experiencing it. It's sort of like someone telling you what it's like to have a baby, but when you're going through transition you realize that nothing can describe what it's like. It was amazing. I could actually feel Mom's hair and smell her room. And being so scared and lost and alone...that's exactly how I felt when I was ten. Confusing too; loving her and hating her...wanting her to live and wishing she'd die. A lot of guilt there. It's so sad to think I had to go through that. Reliving it really brings home how much that affected me. I feel a mixture of awe and compassion, also tremendous relief. But I'm not sure I'd want to go through it again. I'm really exhausted.

The issue of guilt seemed important for Liz. After talking further, she realized that she hadn't really wanted her Mom to die. She understood that the experience was so frightening that she had just wanted the intense feelings to end. Her child's mind had formulated this as a wish that her mother would die, and then it would be over. After discussing this, Liz felt relieved of this guilt.

Fear of Losing Control

This fear relates to the previous fears. The client fears "letting go" and trusting the process because undesired self-disclosures, deep dark secrets, feelings of going crazy, unbearable pain, or never-ending grief may emerge.

Processing the client's specific reason for fearing loss of control is important. For example, Ilene expressed the belief that if she began crying, she might not be able to stop. She imagined her pain as endless as a dark ocean in which she would be afloat in a tiny boat, unable to find the shore again. In this state, she would be unable to take care of her family or go to work. When asked what might allow her to explore these feelings, she said that having a lifeline to an anchor on the shore would help her. She was comforted by a suggestion that she imagine the therapist as her lifeline to help her find her way back from the pain. She was also taught the Light Stream Technique (Appendix G) as a means to achieve closure, in case this didn't happen naturally. Finally, sessions were scheduled on Saturday morning so she would have the weekend to recover, before going back to work.

❖ *Fear of Failure*

This fear stems from performance anxiety — some clients fear that they won't be able to "do the therapy right." Clients can be instructed to say whatever occurs to them, even if it's the thought that, "I can't do this" or "I'm not getting anything." These thoughts offer a place to begin. Usually by focusing on physical sensations or images, the client's attention shifts from judging performance to concentrating on the process.

Exploring the fear behind failure also offers another means to help clients feel more comfortable. One client expressed the feeling that if this therapy didn't work, she would give up in despair. She had tried numerous therapists and therapies and still had problems with intimate relationships. She was counting on MT to solve her problem. Further exploration revealed that she was seeing her former therapy as a complete failure, when actually she had gained a lot from the experience. This helped her relax and focus on the process rather than the outcome.

❖ *Fear That the Therapy Is Not Working Properly*

After a session, some clients may complain that the therapy "wasn't doing anything." This statement points to the client's fear that the therapy isn't working. In exploring this further, the therapist can determine if the client was resisting the process. Other underlying fears, discussed previously, often block the process. Once these fears are discussed, clients may be able to allow the therapy to work.

The therapist can usually, but not always, detect when the client is resisting the process. Long pauses, falling asleep, surface talking and no discharging may all indicate resistance. Reminding clients to describe everything that comes into awareness often starts the processing. If this fails to work, the therapist should direct the client to focus on a limited area such as bodily reactions or visual images. When the client continues to resist, it may be necessary to stop the session and explore the client's fears.

Clients may also complain of feeling worse after the first few MT sessions. The therapist should explore such reactions to determine what the client means by "feeling worse." Feeling worse may actually be a sign of progress. For clients who have compartmentalized or shut off feelings regarding an issue, experiencing these feelings again may lead them to conclude that they are becoming less functional. Pointing out that sometimes they may feel worse before they feel better, helps clients to trust the therapy and continue.

Symptoms generated from cutting off feelings — such as compulsive eating, working, or spending — usually diminish when clients begin feeling and expressing emotions. Pointing out the progress in symptom reduction can encourage clients to realize that the therapy is working, even though they feel worse.

Clients may also need further education regarding feelings and containing emotions. Clients who have never allowed themselves to feel angry may feel threatened when anger emerges. Anger management techniques and closure techniques such as the Light Stream can help these individuals to manage feelings that seem overwhelming. It may also be necessary to schedule sessions more frequently, until such clients feel less overwhelmed.

After several MT sessions, Deborah reported feeling "a lot of anger coming up." This anger accompanied a realization that she hadn't been allowed to be a child. It was a normal part of grieving a lost childhood. From age seven, she cared for six brothers and sisters. Her childcare duties meant that she couldn't join in sports, cheerleading, clubs, dances or dating. As MT sessions processed these years, Deborah's anger surfaced. She had little understanding of anger, since being a "good girl" meant never getting angry.

Exploring the anger, normalizing it, and expressing it helped Deborah realize that the anger was actually progress. She had feared that feeling so much anger would cause her to attack others or "act like a bitch."

In rare cases, the therapist may determine that the client's condition does not improve or is exacerbated by Meditative Therapy. In most cases, these clients should have been ruled out due to psychological, medical or environmental factors such as crisis or lack of support. Clients may have initially failed to disclose any of these factors, but as therapy progresses such information is forthcoming. For example, one client's symptoms of depression seemed to worsen. Bill began to suffer from paranoid delusions and talked about "holing up" in his house, fearing that the police would arrest him. This twenty-seven-year-old electrician was convinced that the neighbors were talking about "turning him in." When these behaviors were noted, he revealed that he had quit using marijuana and cocaine "cold turkey." He had used marijuana daily since adolescence and cocaine occasionally at parties. He also reported previously trying to quit, but had experienced paranoid and agoraphobic symptoms, so he began using again. Had Bill been more candid about his drug use, he would not have been selected for Meditative Therapy. In this case, MT was discontinued and therapy for substance abuse was implemented.

As with other therapies, clients can resist the process of Meditative Therapy. When such resistance occurs, the therapist should explore the client's reservations carefully. The client's fears are very real and will impede the therapeutic process if not addressed. Once fears are verbalized and explored, most clients are able to proceed with the therapy. In cases where fears do not lessen, other therapies can be used to resolve these fears and MT may possibly be employed later.

Key Points

- Client resistance to MT is usually based on fear, rather than refusal to cooperate.

- Clients may experience fears, prior to or during MT, that may block MT processing from beginning or continuing.

- The following six major fears occur most frequently: disclosure, deep mental illness, pain and discomfort, losing control, failure, and that MT is not working properly.

- The therapist's role in dealing with clients' fears include pre-session preparation, education, reassurance, understanding, encouragement and permission to stop.

Meditative Therapy Outcomes

*This therapy has allowed me to disassociate with many of
my conditioned reactions and defenses. It has helped me
clear my life of most of the repressed feelings of my
childhood that inhibited my physical, mental and emotional
fulfillment.*

*I have developed an inherent respect for my health. I feel
better, so I take better care of myself, then I feel better, and I
take even better care. I believe I have the potential for self-
healing and sickness prevention.*

Outcomes such as these, and other reports of success with
MT, allow most clients to suspend judgment and trust
the Inner Source process. Short-term results often
include rewarding feelings and experiences during a session,
immediately following a session, or among several sessions. Over
the course of treatment, clients may manifest improved physical,
emotional, and/or spiritual functioning.

Our clients have reported an impressive catalog of positive
responses after undergoing Meditative Therapy:

Physical:
- relief from psychosomatic symptoms
- regulation of sleeping patterns
- increased ability to relax
- decreased physical pain

Emotional:
- resolution of childhood conflicts
- decrease in symptoms of depression
- decrease in symptoms of anxiety
- decrease in symptoms of post-traumatic stress disorder
- reduction of habitual fear responses
- decrease in problems described by V codes, such as relational and occupational functioning, bereavement, sexual abuse, identity issues etc.
- increased self-esteem
- increased assertiveness

Spiritual:
- closer alignment to a spiritual source
- increased inner-directedness
- increased creativity
- increased acceptance of life experiences
- increased sense of meaning or purpose in life

The Inner Source naturally produces individually-oriented holistic outcomes. Meditative Therapy usually addresses the client's presenting problems, but often exceeds the client's or therapist's awareness, producing outcomes beyond these goals, thereby enhancing holistic functioning. This process occurs naturally, generated from within by the Inner Source, the client's own self-healing resource. The results of Meditative Therapy are not primarily based on either client or therapist insight, or on interpretation of MT material. However, as therapy progresses, these approaches can be utilized to support and augment the natural healing process of MT.

The following brief case examples illustrate outcomes in each of the previous areas.

❖ *Physical (psychosomatic, amenorrhea)*

Sharon, age twenty-two, complained of amenorrhea (absence of menstrual period) for the past two years. A complete physical ruled out a medical basis for this disorder and hormone treatment was ineffective. The onset of Sharon's amenorrhea followed the end of a romantic relationship with a young man and a subsequent "disappointing" lesbian experience. In the following six months, she lost twenty pounds by restricting her food intake. Any one, or possibly the combination, of these stressors could have resulted in her amenorrhea.

Sharon's first MT session, which lasted seventy-three minutes, included emotional and physical discharging dealing with the loss of her boyfriend. During the week, Sharon reported having her period. At this time, she had not regained any weight. Her periods continued regularly for the next three months, when therapy was terminated. (Follow-up was not possible in this case.)

❖ *Emotional (post-traumatic stress disorder)*

Jack, a twenty-six-year-old Vietnam veteran, suffered from recurring emotional upset relating to his war experience three years ago. He explained:

> *I was a platoon leader in Vietnam. During one mission, I sent a man out in front of me and he was killed. While he died, I watched him bleed, but because of enemy fire, I couldn't save him. After I found out that he was dead, I went crazy. I tried to charge, but someone was on top of me and prevented it.*

Although Jack knew rationally that he could have done nothing to save this man, feelings of self-doubt and guilt haunted him. He continued to react to various stimuli relating to his traumatic experience by becoming upset, crying and hyperventilating. In addition, he reported that other pre-Vietnam difficulties worsened after his Vietnam experience. Specifically, he frequently felt nervous and experienced anxiety over tests, speeches and social interactions. His physical symptoms included stomach problems and periodic muscle twitching. Under stress, he experienced heart palpitations and bowel disturbances.

Jack's first two MT sessions seemed unrelated to his presenting complaint. During the third session, after forty-five minutes, he became frustrated and complained that the therapy wasn't working. When instructed to ask his Inner Source for help, Jack saw two scenes in rapid succession. First, he was standing someplace with a blanket entangling his head and arms. He was flailing his arms, trying to get the blanket off. Secondly, he was underneath a dark cloud bank, which entirely blocked the sun. He was aware that it was sunny above the cloud. At this point, Jack underwent an abreaction. He began crying, yelling, and writhing, as he vividly re-experienced the traumatic moments of the soldier's death in Vietnam.

Jack's abreaction was followed by an intense new experience which involved the physical sensation of energy flowing down his body. In his own words,

> Oh, wow! It's like this huge blob of energy, just working its way down my body. I can actually feel it. It's going down my left leg now. Oh, wow! It's unbelievable. Oh, I just feel so good. How could there be so much, must be tons of energy. Now it's starting again, more is sapping out. It's just amazing! I'm just so happy. It's just amazing! Now there's another vibrating, really fast oscillation. My face and scalp are tingling, arms and fingers too. It's all so clear. It's like this fantastic energy, attacking my heart, my stomach. Still a great big charge in my legs. It's like a dam that just broke, comes pouring out!

This sequence lasted approximately twenty minutes.

One week later, Jack reported feeling "ecstatically relieved of my burden." Life seemed beautiful again. The sensation of energy pouring through his body had continued on-and-off during the week, but less dramatically than during his MT session.

He returned for one additional MT session. After fifteen minutes, he decided to stop because he felt that it was unnecessary. According to Jack, his problems had resolved and he was ready to end therapy.

A six-month follow-up evaluation (Appendix C) showed that Jack had maintained his improvement. Under *Very Much Improved*, he endorsed the following items: symptoms of post-traumatic stress disorder, generalized anxiety, and pre-test anxiety. He rated his avoidance of speeches as *Much Improved*, and his shyness and muscles twitches as *Average Improvement*. He reported *Little* or *No Improvement* of symptoms of anxiety while under stress, such as stomach trouble, bowel disturbances, and heart palpitations. However, the rate of frequency of his stress reactions was *Very Much Improved.*

❖ Spiritual (closer connection to a spiritual source)

Lynne, age forty, had experienced a traumatic history, which included childhood abuse, a series of near-death auto accidents, a divorce and a reactive depression, including one suicide attempt. Her depression centered around her belief that she was alone in the world. After her first ninety-minute MT session, Sharon reported feeling connected to a loving presence. During the week, she experienced the following incident. "While driving down the road four days after the session, I heard a voice in my head say, 'You aren't alone anymore.'" She viewed hearing this voice as "very real" and a "religious experience" which left her feeling peaceful. She reported that she hadn't felt alone since the experience. One year later, Lynne stated that she still felt deeply connected to a spiritual presence. She felt that the MT session and the voice were related and these experiences had been life-changing.

The progress of these individuals is spectacular, as are the rapid treatment effects. Not all results are as dramatic or fast as those of Sharon, Jack, and Lynne. However, Meditative Therapy does not lack profound experiences and outcomes. The results and case examples described in this chapter represent only a fraction of the range of treatment effects which have been observed in Meditative Therapy. We have found that MT works consistently, thoroughly, and individualistically, to help clients reach their unique mental, physical, and spiritual potential.

❖ Follow-up Questionnaire

A follow-up questionnaire — Appendix D — was administered to forty-two clients, each of whom had undergone a minimum of four Meditative Therapy sessions. Eighteen females and eighteen males — 86% of the population — responded. The results of this questionnaire summarized here support Meditative Therapy's acceptability to clients, as well as its effectiveness.

The clients were sent a twelve-item questionnaire designed to assess their reactions to the therapy and their (subjective) impressions of the results in their lives. Although MT often involves emotionally intense or confusing experiences, the majority of clients viewed their MT experience favorably in this informal survey.

❖ Overall Impression of Meditative Therapy

Item 1 asked clients to respond to fifteen statements indicating how they felt about their meditative experience, introduced by the general question, "Looking back on your Meditative Therapy experience, how would you rate the experience as a whole?"

Six positive statements received responses that reflect a high favorability rate for MT.

Statement	Response: *"quite a bit" or "very much"*
a very pleasant experience	67%
something I want to try again	89%
an experience of great beauty	36%
greater awareness of reality	67%
feel it was of lasting benefit to me	81%
the greatest thing that ever happened to me	39%

Three neutral statements were endorsed by fewer than half of the respondents:

Statement	Response: *"quite a bit" or "very much"*
like traveling to a far-off land	36%
return to feelings of childhood	44%
a religious experience	25%

Six negative statements received virtually no endorsements; the MT experience was not a negative experience for the great majority of respondents.

Statement	Response: *"not at all" or "a little"*
very unpleasant experience	8%
disappointing experience	0%
an experience of insanity	3%
did me harm mentally	3%
very much like being drunk	3%
physical discomfort and illness	17%

❖ *Effectiveness of Meditative Therapy*

The second item assessed the client's perception of the effectiveness of Meditative Therapy: *"How were you, or what were you left with, after your Meditative Therapy experiences?"* Sixteen statements considered the effectiveness of MT in the following areas: interpersonal, mental/emotional, physical, and spiritual. Statements were assigned categories according to their predominant area of impact.

Effectiveness on Interpersonal Functioning. Four statements assessed the effectiveness of Meditative Therapy on interpersonal relationships. About half of the respondents noted improvement in this area of their lives.

Statement	*Response: "quite a bit" or "very much"*
greater understanding of the importance and meaning of human relationships	50%
sense of greater regard for the welfare and comfort of other human beings	36%
improvement noted by people closest to me	50%
greater tolerance of others	50%

Effectiveness on Mental and Emotional Functioning. Five statements dealt with the effectiveness of Meditative Therapy on the mental and emotional aspects of individuals. More variability on this item but again, nearly half the responses were favorable.

Statement	*Response: "quite a bit" or "very much"*
new way of looking at the world	39%
a sense of relaxation, freedom from anxiety and tension	69%
better understanding of the cause and source of my troubles	58%
set of new decisions and new directions for my life	42%
new sense of fun and enjoyment	34%

Item 12 (*Is there anything else you can tell of your experience that was particularly exciting, disturbing, unusual, etc.?*) allowed for open-ended responses in all areas. Narrative answers that reflected positive gains mentally and emotionally include the following:

> *Before MT all the stress and strain would have been very trying on me, but I feel unusually calm and peaceful under the circumstances, where before I would have been in a frantic state — unable to eat, sleep, filled with anxiety. I feel in control, and little annoyances don't bother me, even the post office, waiting in line to send packages, shopping in stores, traffic, and packing and shipping all my belongings by Greyhound. This is the supreme test of MT, and I went through it all without the usual nerves and tension I have experienced in the past.*

> *I feel that the experience has given me more confidence and a good inner feeling.*

> *I learned how to take care of myself and listen to myself and not to run from my feelings — to relax and let things be. It taught me not to worry. It released a lot of past burdens.*

> *I have become more aware of myself and my uniqueness and have really come to like myself.*

> *Prior to this vision* (MT experience), *I had always been a little freaked out by noises at night, which used to keep me awake. I was paranoid someone was breaking in and I would get up and check out strange noises. After my "vision" and until this day, I don't even listen to noises and never get up or lay awake. I just go right to sleep and never worry about it, which is great.*

> *If I'm feeling "down," I can use this understanding of the various things that affect my overall sense of being to help me find what's making me feel "down" and change it.*

> *As the sessions went on, I found more complete relaxation and freedom from uneasiness. My fears about getting hyperanxious were dispelled.*

Effectiveness on Physical Functioning. One statement assessed physical effects (other than responses to anxiety or tension).

Statement	*Response: "quite a bit" or "very much"*
Colors have been brighter	25%

Several responses from Item 12 (*Is there anything else you can tell of your experience that was particularly exciting, disturbing, unusual, etc.?*) indicated improved physical functioning.

> *First of all, my back had been bothering me quite a bit. After several sessions, it quit bothering me for about six months, and hasn't bothered me near as much since therapy.*

> *I had always had trouble relaxing when my husband and I had sex. The evening after my first M-T, when I had sex with my husband, I was very relaxed and was able to get the maximum out of our intercourse that evening. The next time we had sex, I was not as relaxed as the evening described above, but I have more and more sexual experiences that I feel I get the maximum from.*

> *Much more aware of my physical reaction to emotional feelings.*

> *I am more aware of what my body is telling me.*

Effectiveness on Spiritual Functioning. Three statements in Item 2 dealt with spirituality. Statements related to beauty, meaning, and purpose are included in this area. Many clients reported positive spiritual effects.

Statement	*Response: "quite a bit" or "very much"*
greater awareness of God, or a higher power or an ultimate reality	31%
new understanding of beauty and art	28%
sense of now knowing what life is all about	31%

In response to Item 7 (*Have your feelings on religion and what it means changed any as a result of your MT experience?*), 36% indicated a change. Below are representative responses:

Closer to God.

I am more aware of a spiritual need and belief.

I seem to have more faith in a Supreme Being. No longer the concept of heaven or hell or punishment for sins, but a good feeling and faith in a spiritual world.

Reaffirmed and made stronger (my beliefs). *Belief in the existence of a higher order or general purpose, God. Established the belief that God exists inside everyone.*

I found the source of spiritual power inside, paradoxically, rather than by trying to search it out or find it somewhere.

The world was one. Everything was beautiful. Everything was so perfect. Like I was in the back seat with a driver. I was very relaxed and happy. My soul guided me to what I needed and still does.

Item 8, (*Have your experiences with MT changed your feelings about death in any way?*), results showed a positive effect for many clients. 36% felt less afraid, more at ease, and more positive about death after MT.

Item 9, (*Do you trust God or a supreme being or concept more than you did?*), this question elicited a positive response for 31%. For many this trust was felt as a deeper inner connection to God or a supreme being.

Overall (Holistic) Effectiveness. Many clients noted an increased holistic effect of a greater integration of mind, body, and spirit in response to Item 12 (*Is there anything else you can tell of your experience that was particularly exciting, disturbing, unusual, etc.?*).

During therapy, and since, I feel more aware of a variety of sensory experiences. Instead of one overall "sense of being," I gained a sense of how I felt in body, spirit, consciousness, etc. What I mean is that feelings were differentiated — what

I saw, how my body felt, what I thought — were all separate parts of a composite sense of being.

Major thing I learned to trust my feelings and not just to trust apparent facts and relationships, as I had been taught was the only way. I finally felt like all the parts were a whole.

Through the experience, I gained an awareness of the strong connection of mind and body. One helps the other for the benefit of both.

❖ *Key Points*

- The results of research and case studies demonstrate the acceptability of MT to clients and the holistic effectiveness of MT.

- The physical effects of MT include a decrease in psychosomatic symptoms and physical pain, regulation of sleep patterns, and improved ability to relax.

- Emotional results include resolution of childhood conflicts, a decrease in depression, anxiety, PTSD symptoms, and fear, and an increase in self-esteem and assertiveness.

- Spiritual results include feeling closer to a spiritual source, greater inner direction, creativity, acceptance of life, and sense of meaning and purpose.

9 ❖

Facilitating Meditative Therapy:
Procedures and Cautions

This book seeks to educate interested clinicians in the development, theory, supportive case material, and practical application of Meditative Therapy. This chapter offers specific guidelines for clinicians who elect to add MT to their therapeutic repertoire.

Therapist Preparation
❖

Meditative Therapy should only be utilized by fully qualified mental health professionals, licensed therapists, or interns practicing under a qualified clinical supervisor. This caution underscores the fact that MT should be used as part of a comprehensive, integrative treatment plan. It is expected that the therapist will bring a vast array of clinical knowledge and skills to the successful application of MT.

While some psychotherapists (those who have previous training in inner-oriented methods such as hypnosis or Eye Movement Desensitization and Reprocessing) may be able to incorporate MT into their practices from studying this book, additional training is recommended. MT workshops offer a more complete training experience and focus on using appropriate safeguards, dealing with intense emotional material, supporting clients through abreactions or unusual MT experiences, and integrating MT into the treatment program.

As with any powerful intra-psychic therapy, of course, first-hand knowledge of the MT process is extremely valuable to the clinician. A personal MT experience also sensitizes the therapist to the powerful nature of Meditative Therapy and creates trust, respect and appreciation of the Inner Source process. When clients encounter intense or unusual material, reassurance from the therapist's personal experience can be highly supportive.

Tracking and recording Meditative Therapy sessions provides insight regarding the diversity and wisdom of the Inner Source process. MT sessions vary greatly according to each individual client's needs. Writing down session content word-for-word is worth the effort, though not easy and not always possible, because of the speed with which some clients report. Audio tapes provide invaluable back-up for this task, of course.

❖ Personal Qualities of the Therapist

Professional use of any therapeutic approach requires certain qualities in the therapist. Not all are suited to use Assertiveness Training, Hypnotherapy, Rational Emotive Behavior Therapy, or Client-Centered Therapy. The same is true of Meditative Therapy: Certain therapist characteristics enhance the successful facilitation of MT. The personal qualities most needed are patience, trust, tolerance and openness.

Patience is necessary in Meditative Therapy because of the amount of time required for the therapy. It's advisable to allow sixty to ninety minutes per session. Sitting quietly and recording the MT transcript for this period of time may seem boring to therapists of some temperaments.

Trust means acceptance of the process of the Inner Source and faith that the Inner Source will never violate the client or require anything beyond his or her capacity. Doubts may occur, but if the therapist remains confident, the Inner Source will eventually achieve positive results. At times, the process seems to move backward before it goes forward, but growth often follows that pattern.

Tolerance allows the therapist to remain present with the client during intense or unusual MT experiences. Because the Inner Source may go backward — into "darkness" — before it goes forward — or into "light" — the therapist must be able to tolerate "heavy" or "powerful" material. Clients' experiences with intense emotional reactions such as grief and anger, "violent" bodily movements, traumatic events from the past, and parapsychological phenomena can be similarly dramatic — and often unnerving — for the therapist. When such experiences occur, it is almost impossible not to "feel" with the person. Identifying with the client may elicit strong reactions in the therapist, such as sadness, exhaustion, exhilaration, and anger. The session content may also trigger some of the therapist's own material, which may need to be dealt with through the therapist's own therapy.

Openness is the final important quality. The Inner Source may appear ambiguous or even contradictory, judging from the material being presented. At times, the Inner Source is difficult, if not impossible, to understand and occasionally even seems to produce nonsense. If the therapist remains open and waits non-judgmentally, the end result usually proves worthwhile. Even if some of the material presented goes against one's belief system or background of experiences, it is more therapeutic to be open and accepting if possible.

The therapist who possesses these qualities models them for the client. When the therapist remains patient, tolerant, trusting, and open, the client usually follows suit. This is especially crucial during abreactive or unusual sequences, when clients rely on the therapist for support.

Is the Meditative Therapist Really Non-Directive?

The *primary* emphasis of Meditative Therapy, *trusting the client's Inner Source*, defines the therapist's role as basically non-directive. During MT, the therapist interacts with the client only to direct the client's attention back to the process. For example, if a client states, "I'm feeling jumpy," the therapist simply directs the client to watch this feeling. Directive statements may also be used in dealing with client fears, mistrust, or resistance. However, the focus is *to support the client to stay with the process and allow it to work.*

When using directives, the therapist must determine each client's *capacity* to proceed. The following guidelines apply:

- The *ultimate decision* as to whether or not to proceed, in every case, *lies with the client.*

- The client's trust in the therapist is a necessary prerequisite to using directives aimed at fears or resistances.

- The therapist must remain sensitive to the client's

strength and not direct beyond an encouragement to proceed.

- The therapist uses directives only for the purpose of allowing the Inner Source to continue processing.

The therapist will be most effective by demonstrating confidence in the therapy and encourage the client to trust the process as well. (In this regard, all therapies are "directive.") In consenting to undertake Meditative Therapy, the therapist and client agree to trust the Inner Source. Once that commitment is made, both remain "non-directive," allowing the Inner Source process to work unimpeded.

❖ Role of the Therapist in Meditative Therapy

Despite the non-directive role of the therapist and the self-healing nature of the Inner Source process, the therapist plays an important role throughout the course of Meditative Therapy. *Prior* to beginning the therapy, the therapist: (1) selects clients; (2) introduces and instructs clients in the process of Meditative Therapy; and (3) answers client questions. *During* MT, the therapist (4) prompts the client to continuously describe what is taking place, to be patient and not to interfere with the process; (5) tracks and records the process; (6) handles fears and resistance; and (7) ensures that the session finishes properly and that the client is re-oriented and alert. *After* Meditative Therapy, the therapist (8) de-briefs the sessions; (9) assigns homework; (10) remains available between sessions as needed; and (11) follows up. The balance of this chapter is devoted to an examination of each of these key elements of the therapist's role in MT.

❖ Selection of Clients

Client selection guidelines (see Chapter 4) should be carefully followed prior to beginning Meditative Therapy. While it is our belief that most clients can benefit from MT, restrictions concerning substance abuse, psychotic disorders, severe personality disorders, medical conditions, and crisis situations must be followed. Additionally, the client's level of strength and support should be assessed. These cautions safeguard clients against possible physical or emotional reactions that could not be handled on an outpatient basis.

Among the psychodiagnostic considerations which lead us to recommend MT to our clients are chronic depression, psychosomatic complaints, restricted affect, significant lack of assertiveness, significant lack of self-esteem, history of abuse (past or present), and Post-traumatic Stress Disorder.

Clients should always make the final decision to begin MT. Certain clients may not choose to participate in MT after hearing a basic explanation. In our experience, however, most clients who meet the selection criteria elect to try MT. Those who seem most willing to attempt MT fall into the following categories: (1) clients who are interested in or involved in altered states of consciousness such as meditation, hypnosis, or relaxation; (2) individuals who are deeply involved in spiritual or mystical movements; (3) those who are deeply involved in and moved by religion, no matter what faith; (4) those who have shown an interest in parapsychological phenomena through personal experiences, reading, contact with others; (5) those who are under tension which manifests itself in observable signs (involuntary jerks, twitches, tics); (6) persons with whom the therapist has good rapport, mutual trust, and understanding.

❖ Introducing MT to Clients

In Chapter 2, we presented a mock client-therapist dialogue as an introductory explanation of MT. This conversation should take place during the session prior to beginning MT. What Clients want to Know About Meditative Therapy (Appendix E) reiterates the theory, process, and possible benefits of MT. In addition, clients should be given an Informed Consent form, which they should sign prior to undergoing MT (Appendix F). Finally, remind clients that they can stop at any time, simply by opening their eyes.

❖ Answering Client Questions Regarding MT

It's important to ask clients if they have any questions or concerns prior to beginning Meditative Therapy. This provides an opportunity to give additional information about MT or to deal with fears or resistance that may later block the process. Chapter 2 lists possible responses to a variety of frequent client questions and concerns and Chapter 7 explains the most frequent fears regarding MT. Although most questions can be answered in a general manner, clients should be reminded that the Inner Source process varies according to individual needs and that it's impossible to predict exactly what will occur in their own MT sessions.

❖ *Prompting Clients*

The essential steps for the clients to follow are: (1) lie back, close the eyes, (2) form the intention to ask for help, (3) watch patiently, (4) describe continuously what is being experienced, and (5) allow the Inner Source to proceed. Remind the client not to interfere with the process, but simply to allow it to unfold. The sample dialogue in Chapter 2 details this instruction.

Directive Statements: Most clients ask questions during the initial minutes of the first and sometimes the second session. These questions relate primarily to whether or not the client is doing the therapy "correctly." Below are several actual questions and responses taken from Meditative Therapy transcripts.

Questions	*Responses*
Am I just supposed to experience it or what?	*Yes, and just describe what is happening.*
Whatever I feel, I say?	*Yes.*
Should I just start telling you?	*Yes.*
Should I report what I am thinking about?	*Yes, anything you think or see or feel.*
I'm not sure where to start; right now I'm aware of my body functioning.	*Just describe it.*

Once the therapist feels confident that the client understands and is engaging in the process, this minimal amount of direction can be discontinued.

Supportive Statements. Reassuring and reinforcing client statements encourages clients to stay with the process and continue describing what is happening. The following examples suggest how the therapist might respond in the early stages of Meditative Therapy.

Client Description	*Therapist Response*
My stomach's becoming tight.	*That's okay.*
My face doesn't feel so hot. It's cooled off, but I get this blue.	*Mm. Just stay with that.*
It comes and goes.	*Mm.*
I feel like waiting, waiting, waiting in the fog.	*Good.*
Just noises, tense, colors, different patterns.	*Just describe those.*

Prompting Continual Verbalization. Continual verbalization helps sensitize the client to the importance of seemingly "trivial" occurrences (body feelings, random thoughts). It also facilitates the maintenance of a dual consciousness, i.e., the awareness of being present in the therapy room and of having inner experiences at the same time. This awareness creates greater safety for the client during sequences of intense feelings, abreactions, or unusual experiences. If long pauses occur, it is important to ask what is taking place and to emphasize continual description.

Client Description	*Therapist Response*
(Silence over three-to-five minutes.)	*What's going on now?*
Mm.	*I want you to keep telling me what you're getting.*
Just scenes from when I lived at home.	*I'd like you to describe the scenes.*
I'm seeing the living room on linton Street.	*That's good...what about the living room?*

Prompting Patience and Non-Interference. The therapist may need to encourage the client to be patient and not to interfere with the therapeutic process.

Client Statement	*Therapist Response*
Now I feel shaky inside, I feel like crying.	*Yes, just let it happen.*
Now I have a feeling of wanting to happen, though I know I shouldn't want to force it.	*Right, just be patient.*
What if I don't see anything?	*That's okay, there may be periods where you won't. Just let that happen.*
I feel real small, but puff up sometimes. I don't like the way I feel.	*It may be uncomfortable, but try to go with it. It usually works through the discomfort.*

❖ *Recording and Tracking the Process*

As mentioned earlier, it is important that the therapist record each MT session. Paying attention to the content by recording it also aids in tracking the session. Knowing what types of material and reactions to watch for helps the therapist determine whether or not processing is occurring. These signs may be either physical or psychological. Bodily reactions, such as feelings of falling, tingling, heaviness or lightness, pain or discomfort, indicate that the therapy is working. Mental or visual signs, such as seeing lights, colors, patterns, objects, or past events, usually indicate that processing is proceeding. The therapist must discriminate between everyday waking purposeful thought, and inner-directed thought presented by the Inner Source. Thought patterns provide a crucial indicator of correct processing, and examples of outer-directed and inner-directed thought are given below. The outer example is from a man's first session; the inner example is from a woman's first session.

Outer-Directed Thought

I don't know, I've been dreaming all day, daydreaming about what this teacher was telling me, to put out effort to understand. I tried to force things out of my mind, but it didn't work — like hang gliding, skiing, backpacking. Those were all I could think about. I just can't concentrate. My mind wanders. Last night I went to a concert, then worked on my senior project until about 10 p.m. I understand the process well. And I read about Lindbergh and I bought Centennial, *something important to read when I go on vacation.*

Inner-Directed Thought

I feel bored very often (shakes head). *I see my living room for some reason, I don't know why, and I think about energy. My living room is my trap because I feel so comfortable there. Mm, I can hear the noises outside very clearly.* (Shakes head.) *I see nothing now. I'm saying, "Lord have mercy on us." That makes me want to cry. Oh dear, I don't even really believe, I don't think, and yet I revert to all my prayers. Oh dear* (wipes tears). *I went jogging this weekend and when I smelled the fresh dew of early morning it felt so good, but I wanted to cry then, too* (takes a deep breath, fidgets). *I'm not too comfortable. I say "Whatever comes will come." I thought of mother, father, and some sexual image, very vague. And I cut it off before it's even actually there. I don't know, I'm feeling all kinds of fragments or sentences. The, well, I'm all right. I'm kind of battling inside I think. Off to battle on a horse — Don Quixote — he was fighting fantasies.* (Voice cracks.) *My horse is dead* (starts sobbing, wipes tears, shakes head). *It's all right, it's all right now* (shakes head). *I really feel dumb. Oh, I don't understand that about the horse, I've never had a horse.*

The difference between inner- and outer-directed thinking can be discerned by listening to the content, voice quality, and bodily reactions. In the outer-directed case above, the content was "here and now" and jumped around. Also, the client's voice quality was light and airy and no significant body reactions occurred. In the inner-directed case, the content was "here and now" at times, but evolved into memories and an image of Don Quixote. Also, the client's voice quality was more serious or studied, and even cracked or became a whisper at times. Finally, her body reactions involved crying, taking deep breaths, and shaking her head.

When outer-directed thinking persists for fifteen minutes or more, the therapist should direct the client to restrict attention to either visual images or body reactions. This directive will usually help the client allow the process to begin (or continue) working.

Tracking also entails recognizing the type of therapeutic or creative response as it occurs during the session. See Chapter 5 for a review of therapeutic experiences including discharging, extended discharging, reinforcement, understanding, abreaction, and treatment. Chapter 6 discusses the range of creative responses, including unusual light experiences, parapsychological experiences, and new experiences. After becoming familiar with these responses, the therapist can readily identify their occurrence and note the type of response as it happens during the session.

Tracking the variety of treatment techniques usually proves more challenging. Identifying the methods the process is using creates a greater understanding of the client's material. In tracking the MT session, the therapist gains greater awareness of client history, significant or traumatic memories, behavioral patterns, cognitive belief systems, interpersonal skills, coping mechanisms, defense mechanisms, and strengths. Since the treatment sequences vary from client to client, the therapist's knowledge of a wide range of treatments from various theoretical orientations, and keen analytical skills, become essential.

❖ Handling Fears and Resistance

Client fears account for a large measure of resistance to Meditative Therapy. We discussed in Chapter 7 six major fears that may come up before, during, or after MT, and how to deal with them: (1) fear of self-disclosure; (2) fear of mental illness; (3) fear of pain and discomfort; (4) fear of losing control; (5) fear of failure; and (6) fear that the therapy is not working properly.

❖ Ensuring That the Session Finishes Properly

Allowing a Natural Ending: The Inner Source process usually finishes naturally, without any input from the therapist or the client. Allowing the process to end naturally ensures that the processing has completed and that the majority of in-session disturbance has been resolved. Prior to beginning MT, the therapist should inform clients to be aware of a natural ending and to stop at that time. The Inner Source usually signals an ending through thought, image, or physical sensations. Examples of endings are presented in Chapter 2.

When the MT session ends naturally, the client usually reports positive feelings of relaxation and calm. Occasionally clients misinterpret an ending or decide to end and may be left with varying levels of disturbance. The therapist should check out how the client is feeling both emotionally and physically. If the client feels a moderate-to-high level of emotional disturbance or physical tension or discomfort, MT should be continued to its natural finish or a closing procedure should be utilized (see following paragraphs).

Creating a Good Place to End. At times, due to time constraints, the therapist must look for an acceptable ending place. Good ending places can be located between sequences following resolutions of disturbing material or following rewarding experiences. The session should not be terminated in the middle of a sequence. The therapist can tell the client that the time is almost up. The following questions can verify whether or not a good ending place has been arrived at: "How are you feeling?" "How does your body feel?" Client answers of feeling "okay," "relieved," or "tired but relaxed" usually reflect a good place to end.

Achieving Closure. Sometimes clients may choose to stop because they are too tired to continue or unwilling to face the pain or upset. Most clients can continue and work though an abreaction when given encouragement. However, if support and encouragement fail to motivate the client to continue, it's important to achieve closure before ending the therapy session. A variety of techniques designed to lessen disturbance and put away client material used in other therapies can also be employed successfully with MT. These methods include the *Safe Place* exercise, the *Light Stream* technique and *Putting Away the Disturbance* visualization (see appendix G). After undergoing closure, most clients report feeling much less disturbed and are able to end. In these cases, phone follow-up can assure that clients have maintained the closure and can function adequately until the next session. A follow-up session may need to be scheduled earlier than usual if processing continues or the client feels increased levels of disturbance.

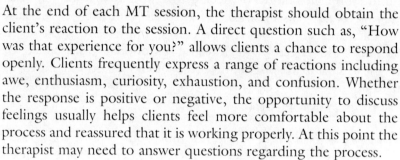

Debriefing the Session

At the end of each MT session, the therapist should obtain the client's reaction to the session. A direct question such as, "How was that experience for you?" allows clients a chance to respond openly. Clients frequently express a range of reactions including awe, enthusiasm, curiosity, exhaustion, and confusion. Whether the response is positive or negative, the opportunity to discuss feelings usually helps clients feel more comfortable about the process and reassured that it is working properly. At this point the therapist may need to answer questions regarding the process.

Another means of debriefing the session is to ask what was most important about the MT session. This gives clients an opportunity to relate to the experience and find meaning in it. Clients will usually recognize important themes having to do with experiences, behaviors, feelings, etc. At times they may share an insight gained from the session, which may include the realization that it's time to deal with an issue.

Finally, debriefing should include an assessment of the client's readiness to leave the office. A rule of thumb is that clients report feeling at least as good as when they came into the office. They should appear present and be able to relate in conversation. Drinking a glass of water or walking about the office helps clients feel re-oriented to normal consciousness. Clients who report feeling physically or emotionally out-of-balance in any manner, such as dizzy or faint, should not leave the office. Usually this clears within fifteen minutes, but on rare occasions a relative or roommate may need to be called to provide transportation home. Ensuring client safety is the most important consideration when deciding whether or not a client is ready to leave the office.

Assigning Homework

Homework helps clients integrate the MT session into waking consciousness. Homework provides an opportunity for clients to work with their material repeatedly at home. In general, the purpose of homework is to facilitate client insight and integration of the MT material. (This important and lengthy topic is dealt with in detail in Chapter 10.)

❖ Remaining Available Between Sessions

Between Meditative Therapy sessions the therapist should be available to answer client questions and to meet any needs for emergency treatment. It is helpful to give the client the therapist's office and answering service numbers and, in instances where the therapist will be out of town, the phone number of another therapist who is knowledgeable about Meditative Therapy. (It is likely that you'll have to work with and/or train a colleague to prepare him or her to fill this role.)

At the completion of the first session the therapist should explain that various reactions may occur between sessions. Such reactions may include emotional responses such as crying; dreams or nightmares; mental phenomena such as flashbacks, images, memories, thoughts; and physical symptoms such as nausea, fatigue, etc. The therapist may say, " *all me if* anything *that concerns you happens. Perhaps nothing will happen, but if something bothers or upsets you, make sure you call me. Once the Inner Source process begins, it may continue during the week between sessions. If you should happen to get sick or if something else concerns you, just call me and we can talk about it.*"

Only a small percentage of clients actually call the therapist between sessions. Most calls usually center around psychologically upsetting feelings and/or reactions. Reactions clients have reported include:

I was watching The Waltons *and started crying, sad to hysterical, back and forth. I felt like I was crying for a lot of things.*

I've been getting flashes of things I hadn't realized before and also crying spells. I haven't cried for years, even after my auto accident, when I had my brain injury.

Two peculiar things have occurred that have never happened to me before. Just the tip of my penis has been itching all day and also itching on my behind. And a big red welt there, on my behind, which has been there since the last session.

I've been feeling depressed and my stomach has been upset. I've not been myself.

*My thumb was really painful, I couldn't concentrate
because of it. Also, my lower back hurt a lot for two days. I've
had kidney problems several times in the past. I've also noticed
that my legs have not hurt for the first time, for as long as I can
remember, when there are severe weather changes.*

Most reactions that clients report are normal and natural and,
as during the therapy, it is best simply to be patient and allow the
reactions to work themselves out. The therapist can offer
reassurance that these reactions are understandable, acceptable,
and helpful. Usually this reassurance provides the needed support
to sustain the client until the next session. However, when the
therapist doubts the client's ability to contain disturbance or the
client reports feeling overwhelmed or out of control, an
immediate appointment should be scheduled.

Not only "negative" reactions take place between Meditative
Therapy sessions. Positive feelings and reactions also occur. After
her first session, a client reported that she "felt a peaceful feeling,
at one with myself, almost with roots again. I feel steady and able
to just be easy, at home with myself." Another said that after her
first session she visited with people more during the week than
ever before, that she was no longer afraid of rejection or
unfriendliness. She added later that, "I don't feel nearly as unsure
of myself as I did before. I feel now all the time like I used to feel
once in a while." Other clients have experienced increased energy,
better sex, beautiful dreams or memories, and a carefree sense of
youthfulness.

❖ *Follow-up*

Client follow-up has not been a hallmark of the psychotherapy
professions but, ideally, the therapist should conduct a follow-up
of outcomes with Meditative Therapy clients. Invaluable
information about the workings of the Inner Source and the
effectiveness of Meditative Therapy can be gained with
appropriate follow-up measures. (See Appendix D for a sample
follow-up questionnaire.) If the follow-up process becomes too
time-consuming or expensive, a random sample follow-up could
be conducted to assess the effectiveness of the therapy.

In any event, the therapist should be available for clients who wish to initiate follow-up contacts at some time after therapy is complete.

Scheduling Follow-Up Meditative Therapy Sessions

Initially, sessions should be scheduled weekly. If possible, schedule a client's first MT session at a time which permits an extended session — up to two hours may be necessary. This may be accomplished by scheduling a client right before lunch or at the end of the day. This is especially advisable when the client's history contains significant amounts of trauma. Although sessions may vary, the first session provides a good indicator of how the process will work for this individual.

The first five MT sessions should be scheduled consecutively, without long intervals between sessions. Especially during the early stages, continuity is important. Therefore, MT should not begin right before a vacation. Interruptions of two weeks or more are acceptable after the individual has a good working knowledge of the process.

Warning Clients about Pre-session Anxiety

At the end of the first session, the therapist should mention the possibility of a pre-session buildup of anxiety or pressure just prior to the next session. The Inner Source will often begin preparing material in advance. For example, Kerrie (Chapter 12) felt so heavy that she could hardly climb the stairs to the office and her tears appeared "automatically" once she entered the office.

Some clients will simply feel edgy or depressed. The buildup can take many forms, including dislike of the therapist, so it is vital that the therapist mention the possibility of the pre-session anxiety. Some clients report buildup, whereas others do not seem to experience it. Mentioning the possibility of buildup is important, because clients who do experience it may misinterpret it and stop coming unless they have been warned. Fortunately, if the client realizes what is taking place and goes through with the session, the feelings usually resolve. Buildups usually become less acute after several sessions, as the Inner Source eliminates problems which have produced them.

❖ *Key Points*

- Meditative Therapy should only be practiced by qualified, licensed mental health professionals or by interns under supervision of a qualified clinical supervisor.

- Meditative Therapy should be used as part of a comprehensive, integrative treatment plan.

- Additional therapist training in MT includes undergoing MT, reading Meditative Therapy, and attending MT training workshops.

- The therapist's role includes selecting clients and providing instruction regarding MT, prompting clients, tracking and recording the session, handling fears and resistance, ensuring closure, and debriefing the session, assigning homework, remaining available between sessions, and conducting follow-up evaluations.

- Consider including scheduling sessions and warning clients regarding anxiety.

10 ❖

Enhancing Meditative Therapy

Meditative Therapy is a client-centered therapy based on the self-healing capacity of each individual. During MT, holographic brain processing naturally and holistically resolves whatever issues impede a client's progress, allowing the client to move to a higher level of functioning.

This chapter presents methods of enhancing Meditative Therapy by stimulating, directing and interpreting the process. While Meditative Therapy should ideally be allowed to work without therapist or client intrusion, if the process fails to begin or becomes blocked, these methods — applied from a client-centered orientation — may allow the therapy to proceed. However, stimulating and directing should be used sparingly and only with awareness and respect for the individual client's history, strengths, and goals. Interpreting MT material occurs only after the MT session is complete and makes use of client centered methods.

❖ *Stimulating Meditative Therapy*

Stimulation refers to methods of provoking an alteration of consciousness. MT employs the minimal stimulation of simply closing the eyes and paying attention to whatever arises naturally. In most cases, this allows the Inner Source processing to begin.

Throughout time, spiritual and therapeutic disciplines have stimulated the inner flow with fasting, spinning, chanting, deep breathing, hypnosis, music, etc. The Inner Source may naturally produce similar phenomena in order to achieve an altered consciousness; clients may experience spinning, music, deep relaxation, or another form of stimulation, as necessary to meet the client's particular needs. The Inner Source produces the most appropriate method, in the correct amount and for the necessary duration, to create the optimal outcome for each client.

However, clients must be able to engage in and "go with the inner flow" for this to happen. When inability to relax and/or low self-confidence blocks forward movement, methods to stimulate the process may be utilized.

In some cases, clients may be unable to focus inwardly long enough to permit the process to begin. This may be due to resistance based on various fears (see Chapter 7) or the inability to relax and concentrate. Several non-intrusive, gentle methods may be used prior to a Meditative Therapy session in order to help clients relax and focus inwardly.

Concentrative Technique. The client initially focuses on a point of concentration. This point could be breath, an image, a mantra, the third eye, etc., according to client preference. After five to ten minutes, most clients will transit naturally to Meditative Therapy. Once the Inner Source process begins, the client can drop the point of concentration and follow the MT flow.

Progressive Muscle Relaxation. Beginning at the head and neck, the client tenses, then relaxes each muscle group (the classic Jacobsen technique): Face, neck and shoulders, arms and hands, chest, abdomen and buttocks, and legs and feet. This method helps clients release physical tension. Once clients feel relaxed, they can close their eyes and focus inwardly.

Guided Imagery. Various guided imagery visualizations may help clients relax. For example, the client might imagine a beach scene and focus on various sensory experiences designed to stimulate feelings of being at the beach. The therapist can develop an individualized script with the client to describe a relaxing scene. Sensory details that appeal to the client can be incorporated in order to maximize the client's sense of fully experiencing this scene.

Music. Since musical preference is highly individual, the client should either bring a personal selection or choose from a variety of selections provided by the therapist.

Once clients successfully experience relaxation through a particular method, they can use the method at home on a daily basis. The ability to "let go" can transfer to the Meditative Therapy experience and help clients allow the Inner Source process to flow freely. Often after a relaxation exercise, clients can transit into a Meditative Therapy session.

Sometimes lack of familiarity with inner experience creates a block for a client who is new to therapy or who may have not been exposed to inner-oriented methods. In this case, shorter inner-oriented exercises can provide preparation for Meditative Therapy. The following exercises are designed to stimulate short, contained inner experiences. As the client becomes more familiar with inner work, these experiences could be allowed to flow into Meditative Therapy.

Use of Symbols or Images. In this exercise, the client chooses a symbol or image that represents a feeling about a situation. With eyes closed, the client visualizes the symbol or image and watches it. Although the client can stop at any time, watching it until the image changes and feelings resolve may be most therapeutic.

For example, Margaret chose the image of a ball and chain to express her feelings about her marriage. As she watched the image, the ball became so large and heavy that she could no longer move. Then she saw herself cut the chain and leave the ball behind. After fifteen minutes, she stopped and processed her feelings about this experience. She then thought of some ways that she could "cut the chain," such as developing some friendships and possibly going back to school. At her next session, she felt more confident to try Meditative Therapy. Her MT session processed abusive sequences from her childhood and linked these experiences with current feelings of dependency in her marriage.

Sand Tray. Sand Tray therapy offers a safe outer way to explore the inner world. Therapists trained in this modality may find some Sand Tray work a helpful precursor to Meditative Therapy.

Brad was initially reluctant to try Meditative Therapy. He had never experienced inner-oriented therapy and was somewhat afraid of its imagined intensity. However, he was drawn to create a Sand Tray. His Sand Tray picture featured the devastation resulting from a train wreck. Multiple cars had jumped the track, causing injured people and livestock to scatter across a barren desert. Feelings of anger and helplessness welled up in Brad, as he described the "derailment" of his life that followed his brother's suicide. Several Sand Tray therapy sessions later, Brad was able to try Meditative Therapy. Brad's MT sessions helped him process the unresolved grief over his brother's death. He experienced some abreactive sequences, but was able to handle the intensity.

Drawing. Drawing the problem or the feeling can help clients get in touch with their inner world. A drawing provides an image to discuss or visualize.

Ann, a severely depressed young woman, drew a picture of a thorny thicket surrounding her and blocking out the light. She sat immobilized, head in hands, in the middle of the thicket. As she visualized the thicket, the thorns began to criticize her for being weak, sick, damaged, and unable to cope. The unfairness of the accusations motivated her to see her stronger self prune away the thicket. She saw herself shred the branches and spread the resulting mulch along the garden path. She then felt the warmth of the sun and saw the garden begin to grow. After this session, her mood elevated considerably as she lessened her life long habit of self criticism. Later MT sessions processed the origins of her self criticism, the childhood experiences of failure and humiliation that had damaged her self esteem.

Dream Work. Dream work can provide an introduction to inner experiences. Since the client is already familiar with the dream, re-experiencing it using a Gestalt approach is usually met with little resistance. The client, with eyes closed, can become various characters or objects in the dream and re-experience the dream from this perspective.

Marie recounted a dream of being chased by a banshee. When she became the banshee, she described being powerful, angry and bent on destroying the helpless Marie. She possessed super-natural powers and flew through the air to overtake Marie, who fled from her in terror. But when she blocked Marie's flight and drew her sword, Marie grabbed the sword and turned it against the bansher, mortally wounding her.

Re-telling the dream as the helpless Marie, Marie spoke of fleeing in terror. However, while running, she realized that she would have to outsmart the banshee. She determined to face the banshee and survive by her wits. A feeling of self-empowerment came over her as she used the banshee's sword to defeat her. Walking away, she knew that she would never have to run away again.

Re-experiencing the dream helped Marie become more aware of the battle between her aggressive self and her passive self. A new assertive self emerged and triumphed. This early dream work paved the way for entering into Meditative Therapy, which she viewed as a "waking dream."

These shorter and more contained inner experiences increase clients' confidence in their own ability to engage in inner-oriented therapies. This helps many hesitant clients trust the Inner Source process and try Meditative Therapy. As client confidence builds, any one of these methods could be used as a starting place for MT. The client can focus on the image, dream, sand tray picture, or drawing and then allow the Inner Source process to flow from this starting place. These techniques provides a link from the known to the unknown.

Directing Meditative Therapy

Directing MT refers to active methods employed by the therapist during the Inner Source process. In most cases, the therapist's directives are limited to the prompting statements described in Chapter 9. These directives encourage the client to observe and describe the process continually as it occurs. Such directives are usually more frequent in the beginning of a session and become minimal as the process unfolds. However, at times, the inner flow becomes blocked and the therapist may need to intervene. At such times, clients may express feeling stuck or may stop verbalizing.

Directing the client to ask the Inner Source for help in dealing with the block may restore the inner flow. An example of this technique is illustrated with Jack, the Vietnam veteran described in Chapter 8. After forty-five minutes, Jack said that he felt stuck. The therapist directed Jack to ask his Inner Source for information regarding what was blocking his inner process. Jack immediately saw himself entangled in a blanket, which covered his head and arms. He then saw a dark cloud bank, which entirely blocked the sun. When asked if he knew what was blocking the light, he replied "Yes, it's about Vietnam." Then a floodgate of emotions centering around his war experience opened up.

Another directing technique helps clients overcome a block by requesting that they interact with an existing image. For example, if Jack's process remained blocked after seeing the blanket, the therapist could direct Jack by saying, "See if you can take that blanket off." This technique helped Sharon, when her inner process seemed stuck in "a grayness with a buzzing feeling, a quiet place of non-existence." This was a familiar place that she regarded as negative. When asked to see if she could bring in a lighter color to this place, she replied "No. I'm out in space. Just nothing. I'm a little pensive. It is my safe place. If I lose it, I'll be destroyed." In this case, the directive helped Sharon's process reveal the meaning of this image. What had seemed like a negative place, was actually a safe, positive place. Sharon ended the MT session with a calm feeling.

In both stimulating and directing MT, the techniques are used only to the extent required to allow the Inner Source process to continue flowing again. In MT, the overall goal is to trust the Inner Source process and to allow the inner flow to unfold without intrusion. The therapist usually acts as a non-directive guide, but must be able to sense when the naturally curative inner flow needs a little stimulating or directing help to continue the self-healing journey.

❖ *Interpreting Meditative Therapy*

In Meditative Therapy, the major therapeutic benefit comes from the actual MT experience. However, the impact of MT therapy can be enhanced through client-centered interpretation, in which the therapist helps the client verbalize and work with self-realized insights that generate from the MT experience.

The activities in this section are designed to help clients work with the Meditative Therapy material either in or outside of session. These activities will increase the client's conscious awareness of issues brought up in session. With additional interpretive work, clients can enhance the impact of Meditative Therapy.

Reading the MT transcript aloud. This homework assignment instructs clients to read their MT transcript out loud, preferably on a daily basis, or at least three times during the week. This allows a re-experiencing of the session while in a conscious state of mind. Clients who experience a high level of disturbance during the session may make further progress in overcoming the disturbance by re-reading the transcript. This task will also increase the client's awareness of issues or patterns brought up in the session.

The emotional response to re-reading the session varies from client to client: Some clients feel little emotional response, others report strong cathartic reactions. Clients should be prepared for a possible intense emotional response and encouraged to continue re-reading the transcript until their reaction diminishes or resolves. For example, one client stated, "Each time I came to the part about my relationship to my father, I would start crying again. As the week went on, I eventually didn't react much when I got to that part." Another client felt a sense of calm in re-reading her transcript. She explained, "At first I dreaded reading the transcript. I didn't want to feel the sadness and pain again. I was pretty surprised and relieved when I could read about my father's death and feel a sense of peace and completion. Reading the transcript was actually comforting."

Clients may also arrive at new insights in re-reading the transcript. For example, Julie reported that "While reading over my session, I suddenly remembered details about Mom's drinking. She'd come into my room late at night, wake me up and cry and carry on about being mistreated by Dad, her brother and everyone else. I can still smell the alcohol on her breath." This memory led to the realization of the impact her mother's alcoholism had on her childhood, an impact she had previously minimized. Margie's insight allowed her to experiment with new behaviors. She explained that "When I read my transcript out loud, I realized that I could express myself more openly. I felt a new sense of confidence. Over the weekend I went to a party, where I'd usually be a wallflower. It was amazing. I was talking to everyone and they were interested in what I was saying. Just being me was okay."

Record the central themes or issues of the transcript. This task is particularly beneficial when clients seem to lack understanding regarding the session. More straightforward sessions may need little analysis, but symbolic or abstract content benefits from this approach. For example, Kim's session presented a long sequence about a bridge. In the beginning, the bridge was sturdy and in good repair. Over time, the traffic increased in frequency and load, placing the bridge under great strain. The trestles began to groan and several of the supports cracked. After the session, Kim was puzzled about the meaning of the bridge. She was assigned to think about it further and relate the image to her life and behavior patterns. At the next session, she said the bridge represented that she was in need of repair. She interpreted the bridge as symbolic of her way of relating to her husband. By taking care of his every need, she was feeling overly used. She realized that she needed to set boundaries and allow him to meet more of his own needs. At this point in therapy, he was a student and she worked, operated the household, and helped him with most homework assignments. This was indeed a heavy load and her symptoms of depression signaled the danger of an imminent collapse.

Make a drawing or a collage to illustrate this theme or issue. This assignment makes use of the old adage "a picture is worth a thousand words." Artistic individuals may spontaneously draw images based on sessions. Henry drew a picture of the Devil that had confronted him in a session. The artistically rendered Devil, confined to an eight by eleven sheet of paper, was much less frightening that the original image. This activity helped him overcome his fear.

Another client, Nancy, created a collage that depicted her emotional response to an alcoholic family. Her MT session featured a box. Her collage showed a young child, suffering from starvation, curled up in a fetal position and clutching a rosary. This image was placed in a box, with a three dimensional lid. Outside of the box, images of darkness, despair and fear portrayed the emotional life of a family destroyed by alcohol. The metaphor of a box as safety, but also as a prison which inhibited growth, became central to Nancy's therapy. She realized that her social and emotional growth had been severely limited by a life-long pattern of withdrawal.

Relate the MT material to past or present experiences. This assignment helps clients make connections between material coming up in the session and events in real life. This allows a greater integration of the MT material into everyday experiences. Simply asking the client how the session relates to her or his life stimulates reflection. Often these connections occur readily to the client, but at other times further pondering during the week may be necessary.

Liz returned to therapy in conflict. She wanted to have a baby, but her partner was unwilling. After talking over the issue, she became aware of some deeper feelings surrounding the issue and decided to do a MT session. During the session, she re-experienced childhood memories of attempting to take care of her father, who suffered from major depression. She never felt "good enough" to "make him better." This sequence was followed by scenes of the frustration of parenting her five-year-old, who recently began screaming "I hate you," whenever he didn't get his way. After the session, Liz related these sequences to the need to "start over and do it right." She laughed when she made this connection to her motivation to have another baby. At the next session, she stated that her desire to become pregnant had lessened and that she had relaxed about the whole issue. Not surprisingly, as she became less determined, her partner became more open to the idea.

Sometimes, the client seems mystified by the MT content. Gina's session depicted a woman lying in a fetal position on the floor, mumbling something indiscernible. Feelings of deep sadness and hopelessness accompanied the image. When asked how this image related to her life, she couldn't say. The following week, she made a connection between this image and her inability to speak up. When her husband failed to listen to or understand her, she felt a similar sadness. Her MT image of helplessness related to her inability to stand up and speak out. She recognized that her depression stemmed from her lack of assertiveness.

In the case of physical or emotional discharging, clients may need reassurance that this is the body's way of healing from past traumas. Betty's MT sessions seemed almost exclusively to focus on physical discharging. Tension in her shoulders and back, discomfort in her arms and wrists, and sharp abdominal pains dominated the first hour of each session. After an hour, her body felt comfortable and relaxed. No apparent theme or content accompanied the discharging. When asked how this might relate to her life, she connected the physical sensations to a date rape that happened as a teenager. During the rape, she had been held down by her wrists on a hardwood floor. Although she didn't have a visual image of this experience, the physical sensations reminded her of the event.

Record dreams. Keeping a dream journal can also enhance the impact of Meditative Therapy. Dream recall often increases during the weeks of MT sessions. Jim's sessions often went back to childhood events which resulted in feelings of abandonment. Recurrent dreams featured a theme of helping an injured child. In one dream, he skied down the mountain during a blizzard and came upon a young boy who had collided with a tree. He left the unconscious child on the slope and went for help. In another dream, he was hiking on a mountain trail when he met a child with a broken leg. He improvised a splint and carried the child back for help. Jim viewed these dreams as evidence of the connection he was making with feelings from childhood. He noticed that the second dream reflected less injury and a more active role on his part in helping the child.

Journaling. Journaling teaches clients to reflect on thoughts, feelings and events during the week between sessions. Eva, from Chapter 2, realized from MT sessions that she used binge eating to avoid feelings. She agreed to maintain a journal of her feelings prior to binge eating. Her entries helped her uncover emotional reactions to various events. The following entry was recorded while on a vacation staying with a friend. Late at night she felt the urge to eat an entire bag of miniature Snickers Bars. According to the agreement, she wrote this in her journal first:

I'm thinking about eating the Snickers Bars... sweet, soothing. Fill up the hole. It's wanting to feel comfortable. Not feeling comfortable here. Why is that? Can't wear shoes in the house. Heather told me to write my letters at the table instead of sitting at the couch for fear that I'd get ink on the couch. She controls the thermostat. It was so hot I could barely sleep. No food in the fridge and she didn't take time off work like she said she would. It's the feeling that "I don't count. I'm not important." That's a thought... the feeling is anger... and... sadness. I don't feel as close to Heather. We've been friends for a long time, but we've drifted apart. I don't like losing anyone, but that happens. Actually, I don't like her that much anymore.

After writing, Eva often felt the craving for sweets diminish and she could stop herself from bingeing. Journaling helped her get in touch with her feelings, so that she didn't need to literally "stuff" them. From a previous MT session, Eva realized that the hole was created when her mother died and her sense of wholeness was destroyed. As a child, eating was her primary means of soothing herself. Journaling helped her change this pattern.

Notice and record any changes that occur in behaviors, thoughts, and feelings. Noting these changes seems to reinforce them. For example, Gina, the client example of helplessness mentioned above, noticed that she was speaking up more. At first she worried that she might sound aggressive and that people would recoil from her. After several weeks, she saw that most people seemed to accept her newfound assertiveness. This reinforced her efforts at speaking up. Jim, the client whose dream journal helped him recognize feelings from childhood, noticed that he was relating to his young son differently. He spent more time with him and reported feeling a deeper connection with him. He related this to his increased connection with his own inner child.

Investigate incomplete areas or issues. Clients often spontaneously seek out more information about a past experience. For example, after a session featuring an extended re-experiencing of a former residence, the client made a trip in order to check out some of the specific details that occurred during MT. Another client, who relived a birth experience in therapy, checked out the details with his mother. The two accounts matched quite closely, although he claimed that he hadn't previously known the details. In these cases, the clients had greater trust in the process and were able to engage in Meditative Therapy more fully after investigating their experiences.

This activity may also yield other therapeutic benefits. For example, Jill, who suffered from endometriosis, felt a great deal of shame surrounding her disorder. Her MT sessions dealt with sequences of growing up with four other sisters and a father who had always wanted a son. She had received the unspoken message that being a female was undesirable. Therefore, "female problems" were shameful. Jill was encouraged to talk to her sisters about their experiences and feelings about being female. Much to Jill's surprise, she learned that two of her sisters had undergone hysterectomies for uterine cancer and one other sister had endometriosis. All had suffered in silence. Under Jill's initiation, they began sharing feelings about their childhood. This helped Jill feel less alone and also more normal.

Read books regarding issues raised in MT. Bibliotherapy offers another means of enhancing MT results. Books relating to session content may offer further insight into problem areas. The motivation for reading should come from the client, who may voice an interest or curiosity about a certain topic. In such cases, the therapist can recommend several appropriate titles.

Key Points

- Stimulating and directing the MT process should only be used when the process fails to begin or becomes blocked.

- Stimulation techniques help clients relax and enter into the inner flow.

- Directing methods help clients overcome blocks in order to restore the inner flow.

- Interpreting techniques are client-centered and help clients integrate the MT material into consciousness and arrive at personal meaning and insight into their MT session.

The Holistic Map

Since Meditative Therapy is comprehensive and holistic in nature, the process often uncovers tremendous amounts of intrapsychic material. We have created the Holistic Map described in this chapter as a means to help both therapists and clients to organize this material.

The Holistic Map offers a graphic representation of emotionally relevant experiences, helping clients to understand the connections among their thoughts, feelings, physical sensations, and behaviors, as they relate to *past experiences, current negative responses* and *current positive responses*. The therapist can help the client fill in the map over several sessions, using the client's history, self-talk, MT material, and other relevant sources of information.

Filled in with the individual client's specific data, the map provides an overview of the client's internal and external holistic responses to past and present events. Clients who understand the map can use it outside of session to trace a particular current negative response to its past source. Clients can also use the map to move from a negative (unhealthy) response to a positive (healthy) coping response.

We have found the map to be an invaluable tool both in and out of session.

The map divides the client's life experiences into three columns: *present negative responses, past core events, issues and needs* (positive and negative), and *present positive responses*.

Figure 11-2			Holistic Map
Current Negative Responses	**Past Experiences**		**Current Positive Experiences**
Negative Events	Negative Core Events	Positive Core Events	Positive Events
Negative Thoughts			Positive Thoughts
Negative Feelings	Negative Core Issues	Positive Core Strengths	Positive Feelings
Negative Behaviors			Positive Behaviors
Negative Physical Sensations	Core Unmet Needs	Core Met Needs	Positive Physical Sensations
Negative Spiritual Responses			Positive Spiritual Responses

❖ *Current Negative Responses*

The far left-hand column lists negative responses in terms of *events, thoughts, feelings, behaviors, physical sensations,* and *spiritual responses.* These initially consist of the symptoms or complaints that clients bring to therapy. As therapy progresses, the therapist can identify more negative responses. MT sessions reveal many more negative responses than clients notice or report.

Negative Events. When clients come to a weekly session, they report these upsetting events or situations: A boss was critical, a spouse was emotionally remote and preoccupied with work, a child was having difficulty in school, etc. Although these events may realistically be upsetting, the client's reaction is more intense than the situation warrants. Due to this negative response, the client feels unable to deal with these situations successfully.

Through therapy, the client gradually begins to understand the deeper issues that undergird negative responses to everyday life events. Current events "trigger" the client's painful past events and core issues, because they metaphorically represent past issues. For example, the critical boss represents the critical parent that the client could never please.

The map can help clients decode their current negative responses to negative events. Once the client can decode a particular response, the negative feelings, sensations, and thoughts usually lessen and the client experiences an increased ability to move into positive coping responses.

Negative Thoughts. A full list of negative cognitions is given in *Eye Movement Desensitization and Reprocessing* (Shapiro, 1995, page 363). They include some of the following self-limiting and self-denigrating statements that clients make about themselves:

> *I'm an outsider.*
> *I can't take care of myself.*
> *I'm powerless.*
> *It's not okay to show my emotions.*
> *I'm worthless.*

The therapist can help clients identify negative thoughts by asking what negative beliefs they have about themselves. As clients bring up upsetting events, the therapist can ask "What are you saying about yourself in this situation?" If a client cannot identify the negative self-statement, the therapist can suggest a variety of possible negative statements that may apply for this individual. This helps the client to recognize a statement that reflects his or her own negative belief.

Negative Feelings. These include whatever feelings clients find disturbing, such as sadness, grief, shame, embarrassment, loneliness, despair, hopelessness, irritation, anger, rage, confusion, and numbness. It's useful to have a chart or list available for those clients who have difficulty identifying feelings.

Negative Behaviors. These include any behaviors which negatively affect either the client or those in relationship to the client. The therapist can initially ask "What behaviors do you do that are a problem for you or others in your life?" Such negative behaviors include *addictive behaviors*, such as substance abuse, gambling, over-spending, shoplifting, binge eating, compulsive eating, sexual addictions; *aggressive or abusive behaviors*, such as yelling, hitting, name calling; *withdrawal behaviors*, in the form of sleeping, staying at home, refusing to communicate, etc. Initially, the client may report a major behavioral problem such as binge eating. MT sessions will usually provide many more examples of negative behavioral responses.

Negative Physical Sensations. These responses are transitory physical sensations that occur when clients feel upset. Some typical responses include tension headaches, nausea, rapid heart beat, numbness, and tightness in the throat. The client may experience a range of intensity of feeling, from being slightly bothered by the sensation to being overwhelmed.

Negative Spiritual Responses. We use the word *spiritual* to refer issues concerning life's meaning or purpose, inner wholeness and connection, and recognition and connection with a higher power.

Negative spiritual responses may deal with despair, guilt, or conflict in any of these three areas.

For example, Betty felt a sense of despair regarding the meaning of life, which she verbalized as "What's the point?" A physician, who devoted much of his early adult life to establishing his practice felt a vague sense of incompleteness. By mid-life, he confronted his inner turmoil, wondering "Is this it? I feel like there's more to me than this, but I just can't figure out what." The adult child of holocaust survivors reported feeling a lack of trust in a God who could allow the concentration camp atrocities. Another client struggled with making a break with her Seventh-Day Adventist upbringing. She longed for a greater sense of connection with God, which her church no longer provided.

❖ *Negative Past Experiences*

Negative Core Events. These events consist of the top traumatic or disturbing memories from childhood. They range from acute, one-time events such as an illness or accident, to chronic, reoccurring situations, such as difficulty learning or living with an alcoholic parent. At times, clients fail to mention significant events that surface later during MT sessions.

Negative Core Issues. Core Issues reflect the patterns or dynamics of the client's core negative events. For example, a parent is frequently late or forgets to pick up her child after school. This leads to the core issue of abandonment. Later in life, the client reacts to any perceived abandonment, such as a husband working late, or a friend not having time for a phone conversation. Other core issues involve danger, powerlessness, incompetence, and worthlessness.

Core Unmet Needs. Each core issue reflects an unmet need. Maslow's (1968) hierarchy of needs identifies the following needs: physiologic needs, safety needs, belonging needs, esteem needs, and self-actualization needs. When a basic need goes unmet, the individual often repeatedly attempts to escape the resulting negative feelings through negative behaviors. This becomes a vicious cycle, since the negative behaviors fail to fulfill the unmet need. For example, the client with an unmet need for love and attention, behaves helplessly so that her husband will be forced to pay attention to her. However, the husband becomes annoyed by her helplessness and then rejects her, intensifying her feelings of loneliness and separation. Becoming aware of unmet needs allows clients to choose more positive means of meeting these needs.

❖ Positive Past Experiences

Positive Core Events. These are the major positive memories that clients report about the best times in their lives. They concern times when the client may have felt loved, admired, supported, understood, or successful.

Positive Core Strengths. Positive memories usually reveal positive beliefs about the self. For example, the client who has fond memories of family trips to the lake may associate these times with feeling lovable, included and worthwhile. The client who remembers teaching her dad to water-ski may report a positive self-statement, such as "I'm competent and caring." Assessing the client's strengths allows therapy to build on these positive attributes.

Core Met Needs. In looking over their lives, clients cite which needs they feel have been fairly consistently met, or met for a specific time period. For example, a client might report that physical needs for shelter, food, safety, and protection have been met consistently. Another client might state that while living with a grandmother, she felt loved and nurtured.

❖ Current Positive Responses

It is equally important for clients to become aware of current positive responses. Tracking these responses helps strengthen them. The goal in dealing with negative responses (left-hand column) is to move to understanding (the middle column) and then to positive responses (the right-hand column).

Positive Events. These are the daily events that clients might overlook or not bring up in therapy, because they aren't part of "the problem." However, they are part of the *solution*. Bringing clients' attention to positive events helps them understand what needs these events are meeting. This reinforces the clients' abilities to meet their own needs, which increases self-esteem and a sense of personal empowerment.

Positive Thoughts. These thoughts are positive self-statements that clients formulate as a result of positive events. For example, the client who receives a call from her grown daughter may say "I'm lovable." When the boss compliments him, the client might think "I'm valuable."

Positive Feelings. In this box, clients record the positive feelings experienced during the week, such as joy, contentment, pride, etc.

Positive Behaviors. These behaviors involve any positive actions which meets a client's needs. Such behaviors include such self-care such as exercise, eating well, relaxation (getting a massage, taking a hot bath), learning (classes, lectures, books), entertainment (plays, sports, movies) and spiritual activities such as meditation, prayer or positive affirmations. Positive behaviors also include support activities such as relating to friends, belonging to groups and attending therapy. This list can be individualized to include whatever positive behaviors each client can name to meet specific needs. The therapist eventually can help the client expand and use this list of positive behaviors. The goal, of course, is to replace negative behaviors with positive behaviors.

Positive Physical Sensations. These reactions include physical sensations such as relaxation, excitement, and pleasure. Becoming aware of the body during these positive sensations helps clients to return to these states.

Positive Spiritual Responses. Positive spiritual responses reflect an enhanced sense of life's meaning or purpose, inner connection and wholeness, and knowledge or experience of a higher power. Clients report feelings of inspiration, joy, security, peace of mind, and guidance.

For example, Mary stated that "I'm not particularly religious, but I have a deep faith and trust that I'm on the right path." John, a regular meditator, said that "meditating provides an anchor for me in a turbulent world. No matter what is going on around me, I can drop down into a sense of calm and peace.

❖ *Eva's Holistic Map*

Eva offers a useful case to illustrate how the map works. Originally referred to therapy by her physician to overcome binge eating, Eva had gained thirty pounds in the past year. A complete history revealed multiple early traumatic losses, including the death of her mother when Eva was five, an alcoholic father, placement in a foster home (with subsequent neglect and starvation), separation from her siblings to accomplish a new placement, removal from a successful placement after five years, and return to her father's home. As an adult, Eva married twice, but both relationships ended in divorce. She reported that she had never had children, fearing she might die and leave them without a mother. When Eva entered therapy, she had little understanding of how these losses had affected her emotionally, cognitively, physically, and behaviorally.

Eight MT sessions provided additional information for her map and developed connections between her core negative experiences, her core issues and her present negative reactions to current life events. The MT sessions also pointed out Eva's needs and suggested new positive coping behaviors. Excerpts from her MT sessions appear in italics to illustrate the contribution of MT to her Holistic Map.

Figure 11-2			*Eva's Holistic Map*

Current Negative Responses	Past Experiences		Current Positive Experiences
Negative Events 1. E. feels excluded in a meeting 2. E. is left alone in classroom at end of day when students leave 3. E. learns that student is removed from home	**Negative Core Events** 1. Mother's death 2. Dad's drinking results in CPS removing children from home 3. Abuse and neglect at first foster home	**Positive Core Events** 1. School success 2. Siblings take care of each other 3. Aunt L. provides safe, loving home	**Positive Events** 1. Friend invites E. on a camping trip 2. Student trainees look up to E as a mentor teacher 3. Principal praises E's program 4. Adoption denied
Negative Thoughts 1. I can't survive the loss 2. I'm all alone 3. I'm not safe 4. I don't belong	**Negative Core Issues** 1. Fear of being overwhelmed by grief 2. Fear of abandonment 3. Fear of abuse, neglect 4. Fear of rejection	**Positive Core Strengths** 1. Hard worker 2. Self-reliant 3. Caring, relates well	**Positive Thoughts** 1. I can feel and heal 2. I can take care of my needs. 3. I'm lovable 4. I can belong
Negative Feelings 1. Grief, despair 2. Anger 3. Fear, anxiety 4. Isolated, hopeless	**Core Unmet Needs** 1. Love (stability of) 2. Protection (from Dad) 3. Food (deprived of in foster home) 4. Belonging	**Core Met Needs** 1. Shelter 2. Protection (Aunt L.) 3. Nurturing (Aunt L.) 4. Included (Aunt L.)	**Positive Feelings** 1. Supported 2. Safe 3. Nurtured, loved 4. Happy, included
Negative Behaviors 1. Binge Eating 2. Verbally attack others 3. End relationships 4. Over-sleeping 5. Shut off feelings (become a "Zombie")			**Positive Behaviors** 1. Healthy eating 2. Be assertive 3. Negotiate, work it out 4. Journal about feelings 5. Seek support (friend, or group or therapist) 6. Exercise 7. Get a massage 8. Create a collage
Negative Physical Sensations 1. Emptiness, gnawing in stomach 2. Tension in neck and shoulders 3. Headaches 4. Numbness, absence of sensations			**Positive Physical Sensations** 1. Relaxed 2. Feeling light 3. Feeling energetic and alive
Negative Spiritual Responses 1. Fragmented sense of self 2. Lack of sense of direction in life			**Positive Spiritual Responses** 1. Greater sense of inner wholeness 2. Increased sense of direction in life

❖ *Past Experiences: Eva's Core*

Negative Core Events. Eva listed four negative events from childhood. (1) Her mother died of cancer when Eva was five; (2) Her father's alcoholism increased and her mother wasn't there to buffer the children from the negative consequences of his addiction; (3) At age seven, Eva and her sister and brother were taken from their father's home and placed in a foster home, where they were physically abused and neglected. All three children lost 20% of their body weight as a result of food deprivation; (4) At age 8, Eva and her siblings were separated and placed in three different foster homes. Eva's placement with her Aunt L. and Uncle R. went well and during the next five years, many of Eva's needs for love, nurturing, protection and belonging were met. However, Eva's father prevented Aunt L. and Uncle R. from adopting Eva and she returned to live with her father when she was thirteen. His alcoholism continued to be a problem.

Negative Core Issues. Eva's issues stemmed from the death of her mother and the subsequent multiple moves after this event. Her first issue, resulting from her mother's death, is a *fear of being overwhelmed by grief.* When she was five, Eva had few resources for dealing with such strong feelings. As a result she repressed the memories surrounding this event and also developed a fear of feeling any negative feelings. The following MT sequence addresses this fear and suggest that Eva might find a way to deal with it.

> *A sensation of something bubbling up, trying to erupt...a big hand pushes it back down...panic...same thing again. No idea what it is. Its dark, oily, heavy...so old, crusty, bubbly, yucky — nothing pleasant. Gut wrenching old stuff, from my core. Makes my mouth curl...sneer. I'm sure it would make me vomit — it would be so awful. I push it down. Stuff it down there, in the pit, the core. I'm sure I do limit myself. Maybe if I let it boil over, or I could turn off the flame and it would be okay. Scary, I guess... self preservation... self-protection.*

The second issue, her *fear of being abandoned,* relates to being separated, first from her mother and then from her three siblings, her father, and finally from her Aunt. Each time Eva experienced a feeling of attachment, this sense of connection was disrupted by a move.

> *Her death...that's what blew our world apart. Linda McCartny died of cancer. A person can't help it. I don't think she went (to the doctor) until it was too late. She should have taken better care of herself. Maybe it was too much — three children, an alcoholic husband, full time job, business end of the ranch. She didn't sound sad to leave. Maybe she did want to leave. Its like an open wound... deep cavern, jagged. The hole...a cavern in between... steep, impenetrable.*

The third issue is a *fear of abuse and neglect,* which relates to the physical abuse and starvation which occurred at Eva's first foster placement.

> *I have dreams of blood and gore. Waggles' head is cut off, or I cut Waggles' head off. I've never had such violent dreams... evil, violence, anger. It's the anger trying to come up. Angry at all of them... f — them — my mother, my father, the creepos* (refers to abusive foster parents). *Nobody taking us. I don't understand her determination to put us there. Daddy so weak.*

The fourth issue involves a *fear of rejection*, which evolved from not being adopted by her aunt and uncle, with whom she had bonded. At the time, she didn't understand why they "didn't want" her.

> *Mother's Day... I had to wear a white carnation, because my mother was dead. Aunt L. said "This is Betty's daughter." I wanted to be Aunt L.'s daughter. (tears) I'm an outsider.*

Core Unmet Needs. Eva's needs for safety, stability, belonging, and love were challenged from the time of her mother's death. Between ages five and thirteen, she experienced four major moves to different families. Her sense of security was damaged when her mother died and her father failed to provide for her. Her life was endangered at her first foster home, where she was starved. The break-up of her family also challenged her need to belong. She reported feeling "on the outside looking in" for most of her life. When she finally did feel loved and protected in her aunt and uncle's home, this was disrupted and she was returned to her father.

These unmet needs for security, stability, love, and belonging created life-long problems for Eva. She has been divorced twice and has experienced difficulty in relationships with friends, co-workers and romantic partners. She developed many negative coping behaviors to avoid feeling the grief, sadness, anger and anxiety that resulted from her early traumatic losses.

> *I do want a family, but maybe not... not sure I want to do the work. Someone to spend time with, to talk to. Someone to love. I want them to love me. Affection.*
> *Someone who would want to spend time with me.*
> *They would always be there. Listen, question, listen to my response...then respond. There would be room for me — other things...feelings too. They'd love me no matter what — fat or not.*

Positive Core Events. Whereas Eva had some very challenging negative core experiences, she also had positive events both academically and socially. Eva had positive memories of succeeding in school. She was especially proud of her reading skills and felt that books had "saved" her. She was able to meet many of her needs vicariously through literature. Eva also experienced a loving, caring relationship with her sister and brother. This love bond nurtured her through difficult times and she recalled many positive memories with her siblings. Eva also valued the five years spent with her Aunt L. and Uncle R. During this time, she felt safe, secure, and loved.

Positive Core Strength. Eva's intelligence helped her face the many challenges of her tumultuous life. Although she endured many losses, she could count on her own intelligence and ability to work hard. She learned early on to rely on herself. This created competence and success both in academics and later in her teaching profession.

> *It happened. I don't know why I have to keep harping on it...why it has to keep me down. (sighs) Aunt L. and Uncle R. gave their two kids everything and they're worthless. They keep bleeding them. We're the only kids who got an education. It made us stronger, I guess.*

Although many of Eva's relationships entailed neglect and abuse, she had experienced a loving, caring relationship with several significant people. Her fears of abandonment were easily triggered and she was highly sensitive to any perceived rejection, but she was able to relate well to others.

Core Met Needs.   Due to her hard work, intelligence and competence, Eva was successful as a teacher. She was able to provide for her physical needs and owned her own home. She derived self-esteem from these accomplishments.

> *I love teaching. When I teach, the whole world doesn't matter — never think about my private life. With these kids — real problems, real kids. I feel that.*
>
> *I'm so into that. I want for them to have success — all my kids — have something that they can hold on to — reading...education. Guide them toward wholeness.*

Moving from Current Negative Responses to Positive Responses

Once the map is fairly complete, it becomes a valuable tool for self-understanding. As the client explores a negative thought, feeling, behavior or event, connections can be drawn between these areas and core issues. Simply exploring the negative issue further removes some of the emotional charge. Once the need is identified, clients can begin to shift to the right hand column and find a behavior or create an event that will generate positive thoughts and feelings.

Three present events that stimulated negative responses in Eva related to her core need for belonging and love. These events represent examples of "everyday" situations that happen during the week, which clients bring up for discussion in session.

Negative Events:

Event 1. In the first event, Eva became angry when Mary seemingly ignored her at a club meeting. She felt tense and made several sarcastic comments directed at Mary. She also thought of quitting the club, although she had enjoyed this group for a couple of years. Later that night, she binged on potato chips and frozen yogurt.

When we used the map to trace Eva's negative responses, she realized that this event had stimulated her core issue of isolation and rejection. In this situation, she needed to feel a sense of connection and belonging with the group. Mary had threatened this need. Eva had interpreted Mary's lack of connecting behaviors as a rejection. Her negative thought was "I'm not valued. I'm on the outside." This led to anger and then a sense of anxiety and despair. These feelings were so strong that Eva felt overwhelmed and unable to handle them. That night, she withdrew and attempted to self-soothe with food.

Using the map, Eva identified ways to move into the positive response column. First she challenged her interpretation of Mary's behavior. She realized that perhaps Mary was shy, rather than rejecting. She decided to attempt to talk about a shared interest with Mary at the next meeting. She also decided to ask another member for support. This friend suggested that they move the seating arrangement, to place Eva next to Mary. Eva also reminded herself that many of the other members valued and connected with her.

Event 2. Eva reported a deep feeling of sadness that had started several days before her session, when the other teachers went home and she was left alone in the empty classroom. She felt a sadness and an unbearable emptiness overcome her. On a physical level, she felt a gnawing in her stomach. She then binged on a bag of Snickers that she kept for student rewards.

Using her map, Eva traced this feeling to the issue of loss and abandonment. The feeling of being left alone was unbearable and she attempted to avoid this feeling by literally "filling up" her emptiness. She realized that she was telling herself "I can't survive the feelings of loss. The emptiness will engulf me." She was able to reassure herself that she could feel the feelings and it was safe to express them by journaling. She reassured her inner child that she was there for her and that she wouldn't leave her.

Event 3. At the beginning of her session, Eva reported that she had consumed a bottle of wine the previous night. She was unable to figure out why she had returned to this behavior, after having a very good week. Looking at the map, she identified feeling anxious and helpless. These feelings had started when she learned that one of her favorite students had been removed from her parental home by Child Protective Services. The student's parents had been sent to jail for drug possession. Eva was able to relate this to her core issue of abandonment, which stimulated feelings of grief. Such strong negative feelings activated her fear that "the emptiness will engulf me." After work, choosing to use a negative coping behavior in order to escape her fear, she drank several glasses of wine and fell asleep early.

By using the Holistic Map, Eva traced her reaction to her own history. Hearing about her student being taken out of her home triggered long-held fears resulting from her own removal from her father's home and then from her favorite aunt's home. This in turn led back to fears of survival and a feeling of instability. Eva needed to feel secure and stable. She realized that she could meet this need by visualizing her "safe place." She also could spend time with her dog or call a good friend for support.

After realizing that her feelings of loss were triggered by her student's problem, she was able to counter her negative thought. She realized that although it might be difficult, her student would probably survive. (Fortunately, the girl had a loving grandmother who had taken custody of her.) Eva also decided to extend more support and positive attention to this child. She left the session feeling more peaceful.

Negative Feelings.   MT sessions helped Eva experience the depth of her feelings in a safe context. Learning to express feelings contributed to Eva's ability to resist bingeing.

> *Feeling hopeless. A picture of me all hunkered down, crunched down, stomach sticking out. Feeling drained. My neck hurts, around here* (throat). (tears) *Feeling hopeless... a picture of me hunkered down, crunched down. I wish I could get it behind me and be okay. I just want to be normal.* (tears) *It's a real lonely feeling, sad, so sad. I'm afraid I'm going to die. Even if they find a cure for cancer, I still think I'll have a short life. I've always known that — not just because of her* (mother), *but also because of him* (father). *He would have been seventy-three this year.* (tears)

> *It wants to pull me in, not let me go. Swirling around and around — can't think. Concerned with staying alive. A black hole, a cavern that goes down further and further — wider at the top,*

then more narrow...If I ever get to the bottom. It has some light in here — sparkles, like stars, but not stars. It wants to pull me in and swirl me around and around, down to the bottom and then vomit me out, push me out. But will I be dead or alive? I'll be out, but will I be alive?

I hate mothers. I hate Mother's Day. I don't want to wish or be wished Happy Mother's Day...Remember how your mother did this or that? No! No, I don't

I f — ing don't remember what my mother did. Anger. Feels hot. People shouldn't assume that fathers may go away, but you always have a mother.

Negative Behaviors. MT sessions pointed out the underlying motivation for Eva's six major negative coping behaviors. Although Eva was initially concerned with bingeing, her sessions brought other problematic behaviors to her attention. Verbal attacks, ending relationships, over-sleeping, and shutting off feelings (becoming a "Zombie") created personal and interpersonal difficulties for Eva.

1. Bingeing: This sequence points out the underlying intent of Eva's bingeing, to avoid the feelings over her mother's death. It is also an attempt to feel whole again.

The emptiness is in my stomach...numbness. I have this one family picture. Everyone is alive, together. I've been noticing it all week. It looks like we were a normal family at home...Mom still alive. I still don't understand how I'm ever going to be whole. Jimmy (brother) *eats donuts. We have to eat to feed that emptiness. Maybe we're empty...fills that up...sleep...donuts... food. Part of my stomach is gone, a big gaping hole. In the picture, I'm next to my mother, so cute. It looks like I'm happy. There I'm whole. I'm three.*

This sequence challenges the use of food to escape feelings by pointing out the negative consequences of the behavior.

> *Life isn't pleasant...everything's a fight...struggle. Body just gets bigger and bigger...donuts at work...eat myself into oblivion. Thinking it will be nice, but it's not. Once I get there...feels worse. Oblivious...Nirvana. It will take me to some higher state...take me away from it all. Lift me off into the light clouds. But then I'm too heavy. I'll plop right back to earth.*

2. Verbal attacks: The following sequence helped Eva understand how her own unmet needs related to her reactions to current situations. This realization helped her control this aggressive behavior.

> *I don't go about it the right way. I pounce on people. I get blinded by hating those parents so much...hate them for the injustices to their innocent babies. I had a kid, year before, his father was an alcoholic. I really had a hard time with that one. Maybe I get to my own feelings through these kids. Maybe that's why I'm so hard on these parents.*

3. Ending Relationships: When Eva felt rejected, rather than deal with the situation, she tended to end the relationship. Although Eva loved her job, being turned down for a mentor teacher position evoked this reaction. Once Eva could explore her feelings of being rejected, she was able to approach situations more rationally.

> *Oh, my God. I know what has caused a lot of this. I had applied for a mentor teacher position. I was turned down. They rejected me. That's what started it. All week I was looking for another job...thinking of running away.*

4. Sleeping too much: This sequence points out the use of sleeping as a means to avoid feelings. During the week prior to this session, Aunt L. and Uncle R. visited Eva. They had reminisced about the past, recounting stories of Eva's mother and her time spent with them.

> *I don't feel strong...feeling heavy...weighted down. Behind my eyes...threatening a headache. My head is heavy. I've wanted all week long to lay the head down. My shoulders are*

heavy...weighted down...heavy...need to lay down. Too much
for me...put it to rest...got to go to sleep.

5. Shut-off feelings (Becoming a "Zombie"): The first sequence
points to the origin of this negative coping behavior. The second
sequence explores the cost of shutting off feelings.

> *Seeing me as a little girl...she's a Zombie...spaces out,*
> *blocks it out. She has to survive. She has to go on. She's*
> *floating in a cloud...looking up at the sky... lost...so pretty, so*
> *sweet, so lovable. I guess if I could make that extension...*
> *maybe Waggles and I could love her.*

> *Feels robot-like...doll-like in the head. Missing out on sheer*
> *joy... Thought I had gotten a glimpse of that, but can't get back*
> *to that.*

Negative Physical Sensations. Eva frequently experienced an
emptiness or gnawing in her stomach, tension in her neck and
shoulders, headaches and numbness during her MT sessions.
Usually these physical sensations related to the avoidance of
feelings and were often paired with negative coping behaviors. As
you look back over the examples of negative behaviors, you will
notice that each sequence also entails one of these physical
sensations. These physical sensations became cues to Eva that she
needed to check in with her feelings.

Negative Spiritual Responses. Eva reported a sense of
disconnection with herself. At the beginning of therapy, this lack
of connection was so extreme that she couldn't remember what
feelings or thoughts had occured the previous week. She
described a sense of directionlessness as "I'm just floating
through life, being blown here and there, not really present."

❖ Eva's Current Positive Responses

Positive Events. As therapy progressed, Eva began reporting
more positive occurrences in her life. For example, she was quite
excited that a good friend invited her to go on a week-long
camping trip. In looking at her map, she realized that this
invitation made her feel loved and included. Understanding how

positive events related to her needs, Eva could then seek out people and situations that increased her chances of meeting these needs.

Positive Thoughts. Eva prepared a list of positive thoughts, which helped her to more easily convert negative thoughts to positive ones. By asking herself how she could change her thinking from "It's not safe to feel" to "It's safe to feel," she could identify behaviors that could support this change, such as journaling about her feelings or expressing them to her boyfriend, a friend, a support group, or the therapist. This helped Eva move from black and white thinking to exploring the shades of gray. Instead of "It's not safe" or "It is safe," she began exploring how, when, where or with whom might it feel safer. In the following MT session, Eva imagines sharing some of her feelings regarding her mother's death with her boyfriend, Sam. The chest contains photos, letters, and other mementos from Eva's mother.

> *I was a regular human being this week. I can handle some of the feelings...the pain. I guess.* (sighs) *Before Sam left last time, he asked if the chest was mine. I told him that it was my mother's. He said it was very nice. I'm thinking, I'll open the cedar chest...share that with him...give him more insight.*

Positive Feelings.   As Eva reported an increase of positive feelings, we noted them on her map. Although MT sessions often provide corrective emotional experiences, this occurred less frequently in Eva's case. However, the sessions did seem to alleviate many of her negative feelings and reinforce positive coping behaviors. This led to Eva's increased ability to feel fully alive and joyful. She actually enjoyed the Christmas holidays, which usually had been the worst time of year for her. Several MT sessions allowed Eva to re-experience positive memories from when her mother was alive. These sessions, although they brought tears, seemed to comfort Eva.

> *She must have been exceptional, to give us so much so early on...to make the good stuff last forever. Wondering if she used to sit in front of the fireplace. I think I have one image of her.* (tears) *I think she used to love the fireplace. She'd lift her long skirts up and get all warm.*

Positive Behaviors. Eva listed some positive behaviors that would meet her needs for love, protection, nurturing, and belonging. Over the course of therapy, she gradually increased her use of these activities. MT sessions often reinforced these new behaviors.

> *Now I have Jenny's family. I go over there and do workouts and I feel a part of the family...not like I'm on the outside looking in.*

> *It's a good sign that I can do so much physical activity. Today, it's amazing... feeling my muscles...strong. Before if I had done that much exercise, it would be a week before I could exercise again.*

> *I didn't believe him at first when he said he had done that.* (Planned a surprise birthday celebration.) *It's unbelievable...no one has ever done that for me before. What a cutie he is.*

> *Being with Aramo* (horse) *is good therapy...makes me feel real good. I love being there. Time just goes.* (smiles)

Positive Physical Sensations. As Eva's ability to identify and meet her needs increased, she reported increased positive physical sensations of relaxation, lightness, and energy.

Positive Spiritual Responses. Eva's positive spiritual responses dealt mainly with an increased sense of inner wholeness. She began to report a greater connection to her inner children, the abandoned, grief-stricken five-year-old, and the angry, rebellious teenager. Although somewhat tenuously, she attempted to extend love to those parts of herself. She also kept a journal during the week, to remind herself to "check in with myself."

Using the Map Outside of Session

After navigating the map in session several times, Eva was able to use the map on her own. She learned that she could start tracing her reaction at any of the five negative responses; events, thoughts, feelings, sensations, or behaviors. Eva often used the map as she journaled about a negative event that had happened during her day. The following journal entry illustrates Eva's use of the map to process her feelings about her boyfriend, Sam, leaving for a month on a job assignment. Eva began dating Sam about five weeks prior to his leaving. They had slowly become closer emotionally, and Eva was allowing herself to open up to him. Here is an excerpt from her journal:

Just finished thirty minutes of relaxation and I do feel relaxed. What feelings am I having? Felt sad last night at Sam leaving for such a long period of time. I did some of my positive coping strategies, but I was still short with him. I have my map out now. Loss, abandonment, alone, rejection. All my core issues are being triggered by his leaving. Feels like none of my core needs (belonging, loved, valued) *will be met during his absence. My negative thoughts were and are: "I'm on the outside." "I'm on my own." "I can't bear the emptiness." Along with anger, I'm feeling sadness, helplessness and fear of being alone again. Negative behaviors: build a wall* (I found fault with him, attacked, then sought reassurance on couch at end of evening.) *Then I just wanted to end it. Tonight I'm wanting to binge on frozen yogurt. Instead, what positive thoughts can I have? I can and will reach out to others...I'm making lots of plans for the month already. I can feel a sense of belonging with my friends. More friends want to be with me all the time. Also I have you* (therapist) *to help me through this. I know I'm connected, valued, and loved by my friends. Jenny said I could call her any time, day or night. I know there are others who feel the same way. I know I can take care of myself. These thoughts make me feel protected, supported, safe, happy, content and included. Behaviors: Waggles* (dog) *and I will take a walk now. I can communicate some of these feelings to Sam and already have to friends. I'm eating well and just treated myself to a carrot and celery juice. Tonight I'll do a light stream exercise and reassure my inner children that I won't ever leave them.*

Using the Holistic Map during the week helped Eva either resist or stop her negative coping behaviors. After writing in her journal about her feelings and understanding their underlying dynamics, she was often able to select a positive coping behavior.

In this manner, the map also prompted her to move toward positive strategies for getting her needs met.

Key Points

- The Holistic Map offers a framework for organizing the vast array of client information that emerges during Meditative Therapy.

- The map helps clients understand the relationship between their present negative responses and their core events, issues and unmet needs.

- The map emphasizes present positive reactions and reinforces clients use of positive thinking and behaviors. It also points out client strengths.

- Clients can use the map during the week to process negative events, thoughts, feelings, behaviors, or physical sensations. By tracing their reactions to their core issues or unmet needs, they can move toward positive responses that can meet their needs.

"Cleaning Cobwebs from My Mind"
The Case of Kerrie

This chapter presents a case report on a client with multiple symptoms, who was treated holistically. Meditative Therapy was the central focus of the treatment, which also included dietary, cognitive behavioral, and insight-oriented experiences.

❖ Presenting Problem

Kerrie, a twenty-eight year old graduate student, sought therapy for multiple symptoms. Diagnosed with Major Depression and Generalized Anxiety Disorder, she suffered from extreme fatigue and often felt tearful, crying easily for no logical reason. In the previous six months, she had gained twenty pounds. She had trouble falling asleep and felt lethargic and unmotivated to get up in the morning. Easily irritated, she was often short-tempered with her two-and-a-half year-old child and her husband. She had difficulty achieving orgasm and reacted by scratching and biting her husband during intercourse. Kerrie also felt anxious — "an inner shakiness" — most of the time. Despite her continual state of exhaustion, she was unable to relax. A wide variety of fears, especially of criticism and rejection, plagued her. She regarded herself as overly shy and experienced performance anxiety .

Physical difficulties included numerous bouts of influenza, colds, allergies, asthma, stiff neck, frequent indigestion, and constant pain in her teeth. (A dental exam revealed an abscessed tooth which was treated.) In addition she became cold very easily. She had a congenital growth on her kidney that became infected periodically. Despite this extensive physical symptomatology, her physician had ruled out any medical problems that might contribute to depression or anxiety.

149

History: Key Traumatic Events

Kerrie's history revealed the following traumatic or disturbing events:

1. Chronic illness as a child: asthma, allergies, colds, ear infections, and strep throat
2. Problems with reading and math in elementary school
3. Death of her father (age 16)
4. Stomach ulcer (age 16)
5. Drug reaction during pregnancy
6. Frustrations in parenting her daughter

Therapeutic Invervention

Diet. Kerrie's eating habits were erratic. In an effort to lose weight, she often dieted; she ate only a salad for lunch and either skipped dinner or ate lightly. In the evenings, she dealt with her food cravings by eating candy or chain smoking.

Kerrie was instructed to establish regular eating habits with three meals each day and an afternoon snack. She decided to follow a high-protein, low-carbohydrate diet and to eliminate sweets.

Meditative Therapy. Kerrie underwent nine Meditative Therapy Sessions. Figure 12-1 presents a content analysis of Kerrie's Meditative Therapy experience. A typical example from her transcripts is given to illustrate each theme. The themes are presented according to the number of times they came up throughout the therapy. Childhood experiences, particularly school problems, were predominant, but problems in parenting her daughter were nearly as frequent. Other important themes entailed her father's death, her pregnancy and the birth of her child, and her past physical illnesses. These themes relate to her list of the five most disturbing events in her life.

Therapeutic Experiences

Abreaction. During the first 55 minute MT session, Kerrie experienced an abreaction centering around her father's death. She visualized these events with deep emotional feeling, crying,

---

Figure 12-1   *The Case Of Kerrie*

Predominant Meditative Therapy Themes
with Examples

Meditative Therapy Theme	Examples/Session
1. Childhood	*In an elementary school-in a green and brown dress, 1st or 2nd grade, in the morning, I'm supposed to be writing, everyone else is finished-now we're trying to read, I can't read either, so I just make things up by the picture.*(#6)
2. Parenting Problems	*I ask C to do something. Then I decide she can't do it, and then she wants to try and can't I get irritated. She's getting confused.* (#5)
3. Pregnancy-Childbirth	*Oh!* (jumps) *Oh! I thought I was floating. It's a hospital room again* (breathing and sighing heavily). *I can't talk — oh, uh, I can't see anything, my throat is all tightened up* (in obvious pain). *I'm in the hospital when I was pregnant. I can see the I.V. and they just gave me that shot and everything seems kind of confused, uh, uh.* (#2)
4. Physical Illnesses	(Coughing) *I feel a choking.* ["Okay, stay with it."] (Holds throat, in pain, rubs chest.) *It's right after we were married, winter time, I'm real sick, oh, uh,* (breathing heavily, coughing), *oh, oh,* (sighing). *It's gray, don't have car or money, no telephone, It's 10° below and I don't want to go outside.* (#2)
5. Death of Father	*Father's death, memories of his life, feelings of loss and grief.* (Transcript was not recorded.)

---

trembling, and shuddering as she reported the experience. Less intense abreactions occurred in session two, three, four and five. These involved prior illnesses and hospitalizations.

Discharging. Kerrie experienced discharging in all sessions.

Extended Discharging. During sessions one through nine, she experienced extended discharging that related to illness, childhood school difficulties, and parenting problems. These sequences moved rapidly, "like filmstrips being pulled past my eyes." Accompanying the visualizations, she frequently experienced physical discharging that involved pain in her legs, teeth, head, and throat. Emotional discharging included crying and sobbing.

Metaphor. Cold served as a metaphor for Kerrie's grief over the death of her father. In fact, after the second session, she brought a woolen coat to wear during MT. In spite of this, she still felt cold, illustrated by such comments as: "I'm still freezing," "It's cold down here," "My teeth are frozen," "Ice in my chest," and "My head is a ball of ice." In session eight, she went through a symbolic death by descending into a mine shaft. After working through the loss of her father, feelings which had remained "frozen" since adolescence, the metaphor of cold finally changed. In her final session, the sensation of cold "melted" into images of spring: "Planting flower seeds," "The sun, it's hot," "Lilacs," and "It's gonna rain…smell the water in the air."

Choking became a metaphor for avoiding expression of her feeling. Memories of not being able to "say what you think" and of "pretending" in order to escape ridicule revealed the origin of this problem. In session three, Kerrie faced her painful ambivalent feelings about her daughter. "Getting a headache…tooth hurts on that side. (Sobbing.) It's about C (daughter)…want to get rid of her…I'm tired." In session five, throat pain accompanied the thought of "I don't want to say that." Then she was able to express feelings of being irritated with her daughter. Once Kerrie could speak out without censoring her feelings, her anxiety began to diminish.

Cognitive Behavioral Events (changing an irrational belief). During several sessions, Kerrie saw an inner blackboard with messages written on it. These messages helped her counter her irrational belief that she must always avoid facing painful feelings or situations. The messages instructed her not to interfere, but to allow the therapy to work and to deal with difficult topics. These messages helped bolster her courage during abreactions and other intense MT experiences. Kerrie fought the desire to flee therapy and bravely kept coming, even though she often dreaded the sessions.

Gestalt Events. Kerrie confronted her passivity by seeing the two sides of herself as two separate people. Although she could be assertive at work, in intimate relationships she became passive. "There are two of me. One's at home. One's at work." She saw her "home self" on one side of the picture "doing things" and her "working self" on the other side "doing things." The home self can't speak out and is ineffective, while the working self "is so precise, just says what I mean." This sequence ended with the home self being hung upside down: "Then I started getting sick. It was like ghosts coming out of the body."

Reinforcement. After abreactions, Kerrie often received reinforcement. For example, following the abreaction over her father's death, she found herself by the ocean, relaxing in the sunlight, smelling the salty air, and smiling. Session two ended with the reinforcement of seeing a camping trip to Yosemite which was "so quiet and peaceful." Her final session finished with a rewarding image of growth: "Air smells different, lilacs... It's gonna rain... Smell the water in the air. Celery, celery growing...growing."

Insight. In most sessions, Kerrie achieved greater insight into formerly unacknowledged feelings. In session nine, she recognized that her attempts to escape unpleasant feelings took many forms. At this point, she has a sense of humor about her behavior. "It was a little different. It wasn't exactly avoidance of the situation, just non-recognition (laughs)." After this insight, she was able to face formerly unacceptable feelings (e.g., not missing her family when she was away on a trip).

Unusual Light Experiences.

Flashing Light

There's some kind of a flashing light — (she jumps) — hurts my eyes — (jumps). (#2)

There's that flashing light again. ("Does it have a color?") I don't know, it's like a strobe. (#6) It's that light, that flashing light — a blue one — it's like in the ocean. (#9)

Seeing halos around people, light bouncing off. It hurts to look at it. (#8)

New Experiences.

Spinning

I am spinning again. (#2)

I'm spinning — oh, it's in a centrifuge, oh — I'm trying to open my eyes and I can't. I can't stop it. (#4)

Sleeping

I feel as if I've had a long sleep, but not really asleep. (#3)

Sensation of cold

I'm still freezing. (#8)

Paralysis

My legs and arms are numb. My arms are neutralized so I can't move.

Falling

Oh! I was going to fall, now I'm falling. (#4)

Floating

Oh! (jumps up) I though I was floating. (#2)

Floating, keep coming in and out. (#5)

I'm floating. (#6)

Time distortion

It's going really slow. I don't mean only slow, I mean really slow... my heart seems to have slowed down. (#7)

Parapsychological Experiences. In session seven, Kerrie experienced an out-of-body experience. "I have to leave again."

This experience seemed to help Kerrie arrive at a different perspective of herself, or as she termed it "an appraising."

❖ *Results*

In order to evaluate the outcomes of Kerrie's therapy experiences, follow-up evaluation measures were obtained at three months and eighteen months after the completion of therapy. These forms included a follow-up questionnaire on Meditative Therapy, a "follow-up of counseling" form, and two self-report measures, which she had also completed when she first came in for counseling. (See Appendices A, B, C and D.) Figure 12-2 shows her scores on the two self-report inventories before and after therapy.

Figure 12-2   *The Case Of Kerrie*

Changes 3 Months and 18 Months After Therapy

Inventory	Pre-Score	Post-Score (3 months)	Post-Score (18 months)
1. Fear Inventory	94	13	21
2. Willoughby Personality Schedule	51	7	13

The Fear Inventory lists seventy-three items, which are to be rated for the degree of fear they cause the person. The scale for each item runs from zero (no fear) to four (very much fear). The highest total possible, if all items were rated a four, is 292. In a study conducted by F. Hannah, et al. (1965), the mean response for 804 Canadian female college undergraduates was 77.90. As seen in Figure 12-2, Kerrie had an initial score of 94, which dropped to a post-score of 13 at three months and then rose slightly to a post-score of 21 at eighteen months. In brief, her reported fear level dropped dramatically and remained low.

For the *Willoughby Personality Schedule*, Joseph Wolpe, (1958, 1990), reported that 80% of "neurotic" patients score above 30. Kerrie scored 51 before therapy commenced. Her score dropped to 7 at three months after therapy and remained a low 13 at eighteen months. Both of these outcomes show that Kerrie's fears and doubts about herself diminished to well below average.

Figure 12-3 is a presentation of how Kerrie perceived herself as changed or improved on her most important complaints.

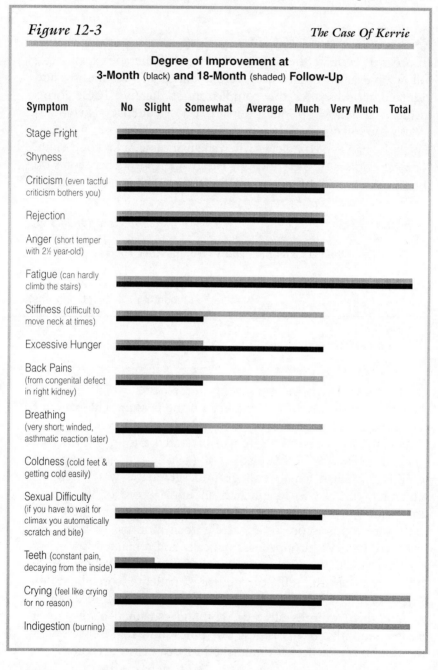

Figure 12-3   *The Case Of Kerrie*

Degree of Improvement at
3-Month (black) **and 18-Month** (shaded) **Follow-Up**

Three months following therapy, Kerrie reported that 12 of the 15 complaints were either "totally" or "very much" improved. At the 18-month follow-up, 10 of the 15 were either "totally" or "very much" improved. Several individual items are of interest when comparing the 3- and 18-month outcomes. First, her stiff neck slipped from "very much improved" to "somewhat improved" and her back pain improvement (from a congenital defect in her right kidney) also declined from "very much" to "somewhat." Her breathing (very short-winded, asthmatic reaction later) again changed by the same degree. On the positive side, we see a significant gain from "somewhat" to "very much" improved for the excessive hunger symptom. Overall, the excellent progress reported at three months was maintained at 18 months following therapy.

❖ *Evaluation of Results: Kerrie's View*

In addition to Kerrie's ratings of improvement in the tables above, which were clearly very high, she contributed additional comments at the 3-month and 18-month follow-ups, and completed the "Meditative Therapy Follow-Up Questionnaire."

On the 3-month follow-up form, Kerrie commented:

I now have immense self-confidence, calm, high concentration powers, greater consciousness in speech, improved logical ability. Also, I have noticed a decrease in sexual desire (contraceptives, I think). And I can relax easily whenever I need to.

When answering the question, *"What was the most outstanding factor in your counseling experience?"* she stated, "The radical change in behavior patterns — self-confidence. Feeling that if I really want to, I can do anything."

Kerrie completed the "Meditative Therapy Follow-Up Questionnaire" again at the 18-month follow-up. The highest mark on the scale for this form is a "3" or "very much." She gave a "3" rating to:

- Greater awareness of reality

- Feel it was of lasting benefit to me

- Like traveling to a far-off land

- More ability to relax and be myself
- Greater tolerance of others
- Sense of relaxation and freedom from anxiety and tension

Those marked "2" on the scale or "quite a bit" were:
- A very unpleasant experience
- Return to feelings of childhood
- Physical discomfort and illness
- A greater understanding of the importance and meaning of human relationships
- Improvement noted by people closest to me
- A better understanding of the cause and source of my trouble
- A set of new decisions and new directions for my life

Kerrie noted the following three items as a "0" or "not at all":
- A disappointing experience
- An experience of insanity
- Did me harm mentally

As you will observe, she did experience some unpleasantness during the sessions. Kerrie stated that there were some pleasant experiences within the sessions; however, the "trips," as she termed them, were frightening to her. It appears, however, that Kerrie was aware of the power of MT and treated it with distant respect. For example, she stated that she would be willing, but not eager to try the therapy again.

To the final question on the Meditative Therapy evaluation form, *"Is there anything else you can tell of your experience that was particularly exciting, disturbing, unusual, etc.?"* she gave the following responses:

Ability to relax, into near trance, but not the same...
Confidence, ability to cope, more sex appeal... Stimulation, can absorb fast... I quit smoking with ease... I occasionally get

"special insight" into people's feelings or motivation... Overall, I have had very good results and I'm sure that counseling helped me. In reading back over this, I see that I got a little dramatic, but the general info is correct.

❖ *Evaluation of Results: Therapist's View*

Kerrie reacted very favorably to Meditative Therapy, achieving significant (and long-lasting) improvement in a relatively short period of time. She had nine sessions of MT, out of a total of twelve therapy sessions. Most of her changes took place by the end of her counseling experience. Although dietary changes helped Kerrie a great deal, changes of the nature she experienced are not likely to have occurred in such a short period of time if diet were the major factor.

Much of Kerrie's Meditative Therapy material concerned problems centering around her past psychological and physical problems. The harboring or storing of residual conflict and pain is often expressed as current physical or psychological problems. This seemed to apply in Kerrie's case. Once she expressed and discharged the pain of her father's death and her multiple illnesses and hospitalizations, her current complaints improved greatly. Through her MT sessions, she also learned to face painful feelings and situations, rather than avoid them. In addition, she experienced the value of speaking out. These tools helped her maintain her gains.

As demonstrated here by Kerrie's outcome, Meditative Therapy has the potential to produce significant and long-lasting changes in a short period of time. Not every person reacts as well as Kerrie did, of course, but her experience demonstrates the excellent potential of Meditative Therapy.

13 ❖

Roots of Meditative Therapy

This feels like the stereotype of seeing a shrink. I'm lying on this couch saying whatever comes to mind. It sounds pretty far out, so I'm wondering if you're going to call the men in white coats to come and take me away.

❖ ❖ ❖

For me, Meditative Therapy resembles Transcendental Meditation. The process is similar, except for reporting everything to you. That adds another dimension. I'm not isolated in my own experience, like in TM. You're with me and I know that whatever comes up, we can talk about later. Since I tend to isolate and do everything on my own, that's an important difference.

❖ ❖ ❖

I can feel myself alter when I go into Meditative Therapy. It's like going on a mind trip or stepping into a virtual reality scene.

❖ ❖ ❖

When I was out of my body, I sensed that I was part of something much larger than what I call me. I felt whole. I thought "This is the real me and I don't want to forget that."

❖ ❖ ❖

As these comments suggest, clients often recognize — during and after MT — parallels between their MT experience and *inner-oriented psychotherapies, meditation, altered states of consciousness,* and *spiritual traditions.* MT actually derives from these four key elements, and in this chapter, we'll explore the various contributions of each element to the development of Meditative Therapy.

161

❖ Inner-Oriented Psychotherapies

Over the years, many popular approaches to psychotherapy have been based on the concept that the human organism possesses a natural ability to heal itself and to grow. Indeed, the entire "human potential movement" of the 1970s relied upon the ideas of self-actualization promulgated by Maslow, Carl Rogers and others. The psychotherapies based on self-healing include person-centered psychotherapy (Rogers, 1951, 1986), autogenic therapy (Luthe, 1969-1970), psychosynthesis (Assagioli, 1971), and EMDR (Shapiro, 1997).

Meditative Therapy most closely resembles natural altered states of consciousness psychotherapy methods. Jung's *Active Imagination*, Kitselman's *E-Therapy*, Frederking's *Deep Relaxation with Free Ideation* and Luthe's *Autogenic Abreation Therapy* have contributed to the development of MT. These methods all access an altered state by focusing inwardly and passively observing the stream of consciousness. However, they differ in terms of the therapist's role in conceptualizing, preparing, directing, and interpreting the process. Meditative Therapy borrows from these predecessors and synthesizes various aspects into a familiar, yet new approach.

Active Imagination, the most widespread of these four methods, is frequently used in Jungian analysis. The three other approaches, all relatively obscure in the United States, include: *Deep Relaxation with Free Ideation*, described only in a German professional journal in 1949; *E-Therapy*, self-published by its author in a handwritten, self-distributed monograph, and *Autogenic Abreaction*, which, although very well documented scientifically, remains little used in the United States.

Active Imagination. This process involved having the patient focus on a "stream of interior images," allowing "spontaneous visual images" to emerge. Also referred to as *Visionary Meditation*, Jung described this method as early as 1916.

Active Imagination uses any fragment of fantasy, such as a dream fragment, to stimulate the inherent imagery process. For example, a dream image of a three-legged white horse could serve as the beginning point for Active Imagination. Soon, by watching the image, further fantasy material would naturally unfold. Joan

Chodorow, Ph.D. (1997), a Jungian analyst, explains that expectation plays an important role in this process. She states that "Such a state of readiness brings new energy and consciousness to the raw material emerging from the unconscious" (Chodorow, p. 6).

Jungian analyst Eugene Pascal (1992) compares Active Imagination to dreaming while awake. During Active Imagination the individual watches passively and avoids conscious interference while the fantasy elaborates. This trains "the ego to be more attentive, more alert to the incessant activities of the unconscious..." Jung said that the process "relieves the unconscious and produces material rich in archetypal images and associations" and that it "brings a mass of unconscious material to light" (Jung, 1958). Active Imagination's contribution to Meditative Therapy is that it provides an early example of utilizing the inner flow, a process Jung regarded as healing.

Deep Relaxation with Free Ideation. Walter Frederking (1949), a German psychologist, developed the method of *Deep Relaxation with Free Ideation* from three approaches: psychoanalysis, psychocatharsis (Frank, 1913) and relaxation exercises. In addition, Frederking's work with the drug mescaline also helped define this therapy. His increasing objections to the conceptual constructs of psychoanalysis and the related dream interpretations motivated him to develop this new method.

Although Frederking's first article on Deep Relaxation with Free Ideation appeared in *Psyche* in 1949, evidently the original research began in 1936. His research was based on a sample of "several hundred" people, most of whom were not actual patients. He states that only a small percentage were significantly neurotic.

In Deep Relaxation with Free Ideation, the patient is guided into a deeply relaxed state. The steps involve feeling the body become heavy, seeing visual images in the inner field and shutting out all other thoughts. In addition, a focus on different parts of the body may be used. When relaxation failed to produce a flow of images, Frederking used mescaline to induce the ideation process.

For Frederking, the patient's experience is the key factor in the therapeutic process, rather than the analytical and interpretive capabilities of the therapist or the patient. He believed that the visual and physical aspects of Deep Relaxation with Free Ideation are inherently curative. According to Frederking, the organism possesses a natural ability to heal itself, once the deep relaxation is induced and the free ideation begins. Frederking likened free ideation to the true dream, in that neither can be "arbitrarily influenced," that is, consciously determined.

Frederking opposed any interpretation of the content of the patient's experience. He saw much of the material as obvious and not difficult for the patient to understand. Certain phenomena, however, are not easy to interpret. Despite this fact, Frederking resisted interpretation: "to break something like this into pieces, would be equivalent to taking away its essence."

In the early stages of the first session, physical changes occur, such as eyelid flutters, heart acceleration or a reaction similar to some current physical problem such as a backache, headache, and so on. As time progresses, other reactions less typical of the relaxed state happen, such as consciously felt changes in body size, shape and/or position. Limbs may seem longer or shorter, or swollen or shrunken. The left limb may seem different from the right. The body may bend to one side, bow or turn, or even seem unevenly heavy. The person might feel a rising or sinking sensation.

During a second stage, one may begin seeing colors, then single objects (a horse, a tree, a profile), at first rather dimly. This stage soon proceeds into a third stage where one experiences physical and visual sensations that may have more meaning.

Much of the material follows themes, which present themselves in various symbolic ways. If these themes are not immediately understood, they will typically become clearer as sessions unfold. However, Frederking holds that *all* of the material will never be fully understood: Some events remain beyond our interpretation.

Frederking's emphasis on the self-healing potential of the individual, which is stimulated by free ideation, significantly influenced our conceptualization of MT. His trust in this process resulted in his non-interference and reaction against interpretation. In addition, his description of the holistic range of response to free ideation, although limited to stages, provided background for understanding the MT experience.

E-Therapy.   In 1950, psychologist A. L. Kitselman wrote a booklet called *E-Therapy*, curious in that it was handwritten and self-published. Kitselman developed E-Therapy while working at the Dianetic Foundation in Honolulu. At first, Kitselman regarded E-Therapy as a new discovery, but later found reference to a similar process in *The Bhagavad Gita* (Stanford, 1970), which dates from about 750 BC.

Aldous Huxley (Smith, 1969) was interested in E-Therapy and describes it in letters written to friends in 1952:

> *The procedure is actually a form of meditation, in which the meditator does not work alone, but is helped by the questions of an auditor. Why these questions should be helpful I do not exactly know. But the fact remains that they seem to assist the mind in its task of standing aside from the ego and its preoccupations, and laying itself open to the central consciousness. In a number of cases which I have seen the results have led to a remarkable increase in insight and improvement in behavior.* (Smith, 1969, p. 650)

Kitselman chose the term "E-Therapy" to emphasize that the part of the mind that removes obstructions may be called by any name. He states that:

> *It has been called the "examiner," the "integrator," the "purifier," (a long list follows)... Since the name to be used depends upon the transient, we shall write "E" whenever this part of the mind is meant...* (p. 4)

Kitselman later speaks more specifically in spiritual terms:

> *So far as we know, it is quite accurate to refer to E as the father within, the holy spirit, the comforter, the witness, or the Messiah. If you regard God as an intelligent, transforming power within you,* praying *to God is equivalent to asking E.* (p. 68)

Kitselman reports only one case in *E-Therapy*. A thirty-five year-old woman became depressed and irritable when attempting college again after many years lapse. She was in the B-C-D range in her school work. Other symptoms were a deathly fear of water, frequent yelling at her children, and slow reading speed accompanied by low comprehension.

The client underwent a total of six E-Therapy sessions. After her first session, she had a feeling of extreme physical and mental well-being, "lost five or ten years of age" according to friends, experienced an elevation in mood, and significantly lowered her irritability. After completion of treatment, her grades improved to A's and B's, her reading speed and comprehension were greatly improved, and her fear of swimming dissipated.

Although Kitselman's methods seem somewhat vague, E-therapy, like MT, shares a common link to ancient meditative practices and a similar belief in the spiritual source of self-healing.

Autogenic Abreaction. Autogenic therapy is actually a series of therapeutic methods developed by Johannes H. Schultz, M.D. and Wolfgang Luthe, M.D., and derived from sleep and hypnosis research beginning in 1905. Schultz published the first edition of *Autogenic Training* in 1932. Later, a vast amount of material including nearly 3,000 technical references and many international experimental studies was summarized into six volumes (1969-1973).

Although the major portion of the practice and experimental work on autogenic methods has been carried out in Germany and other countries, some interest has developed in the United States. This interest pertains to pain control, biofeedback, and relaxation training.

The term "autogenic" means self-generating and underscores the essence of the therapy. Autogenic methods activate brain-directed mechanisms, which participate in homeostatic, self-normalizing or self-integrating processes. The brain, through a wide array of psychophysiological discharges, seeks to re-establish harmony throughout the system. According to Luther, discharges follow self-regulatory principles.

The major portion of the experimental research has been devoted to a set of "standard exercises." These six mental exercises, which allow the body and mind to normalize, include: (1) heaviness; (2) warmth; (3) cardiac regulation; (4) respiration; (5) abdominal warmth; and (6) cooling of the forehead. Research on the standard exercises demonstrates cures or considerable improvement of chronic psychosomatic disorders such as constipation, asthma, cardiospasm, and sleep disorders. In addition, anxiety, phobias, and other neurotic disorders can be effectively treated in this manner.

Most clients complete the standard exercises before proceeding to *autogenic abreaction*, a method developed in 1957, but lacking in research. Autogenic abreaction was designed to help clients whose discharging could not be contained by the standard exercises. Luthe reports that for one groups of 100 patients, 36% underwent four weeks of standard exercises prior to beginning autogenic abreaction.

Autogenic abreaction involves closing the eyes and adopting a spectator-like attitude of passive acceptance to allow the brain processes to unfold. The client must verbally report the content and refrain from interfering with the work of the brain. The process must be permitted to continue to a point of brain-directed termination. The therapist's role involves recording the session, supporting the client during the process and dealing with any client resistance. The brain-directed process is complete and requires no interpretation. However, clients do complete homework assignments based on the written record of their session.

The brain utilizes discharging in its self-curative process. These discharges are usually brief. Luthe identifies nine categories of autogenic discharges (1969 b): 1. *Auditory*: speech, singing, laughing; 2. *Gustatory*: wide variety of tastes; 3. *Olfactory* : wide variety of smells; 4. *Vestibular Phenomena*: dizziness, floating, lopsidedness; 5. *Visual Phenomena*: color, patterns, filmstrips; 6. *Motor Phenomena*: trembling, twitching, tension; 7. *Sensory Phenomena*: heaviness, warmth, electrical sensations; 8. *Affective*: anxiety, fear, depression, euphoria; 9. *Ideational Phenomena*: intruding thoughts, memories, planning.

As one progresses through autogenic abreaction special events take place: 1. *Multiple Images* 2. *Unusual Brightness and Related Phenomena* 3. *Images of Oneself* 4. *Thematic Sequences of the Death-Life ycle* 5. *The Pain rying Mechanism* 6. *The Pain Aggression Mechanism* 7. *Sexual Dynamics*.

Each person's brain is unique and will utilize the discharges and special phenomena alone or in a wide variety of combinations to accomplish its task.

Autogenic Therapy is a well-researched approach, and its extensive and successful application provide impressive evidence of the value of the natural inner therapies.

❖ *Consciousness*
━━━━━━━━━━━━━━━━━━━━━━━━━━━━━━━━━━

Another way to conceptualize the inner processing that takes place in Meditative Therapy is from a consciousness viewpoint. The tendency to identify the unconscious mind as the totality of consciousness and to speak about the unconscious from a negative stance permeates the history of psychotherapy. Freudian lore promulgates the unconscious as a storehouse for repressed memories and feelings which are largely problematic in nature. The infantile unconscious must be distrusted and even defeated, or at least brought under control to prevent its misbehavior. Aldous Huxley portrays this limited viewpoint in the following delightful manner:

> *Is the house of the soul a mere bungalow with a cellar? Or does it have an upstairs above the ground floor of consciousness, as well as a garbage-littered basement beneath? Freud, the most popular and influential of modern psychologists inclined to the bungalow-with-basement view of human nature. It was only to be expected; for Freud was a doctor and, like most doctors, paid more attention to sickness than to health. His primary concern was with the subterranean rats and black beetles, and with all the ways in which a conscious ego may be disturbed by the bad smells and the vermin below stairs* (White, 1972, p. 34).

The "below stairs" portion of the mind which primarily concerned Freud might be called the *subconscious*, whereas the "upstairs" Huxley refers to could be termed the *higher unconscious* or the *super conscious*.

In the field of psychology, three great thinkers have explored the realms of higher consciousness. Italian psychiatrist, Roberto Assagioli, speaks of this super conscious realm in his book, *Psychosynthesis* (1971). For Assagioli, the higher unconsciousness is home to the spiritual self or higher self. Experiencing the spiritual self leads to "a sense of freedom, of expansion." Victor Frankl (1960) views this higher part of each person as a spiritual unconscious. Carl Jung's concept of self also allows for an expanded view of consciousness. For Jung, the self, the totality of conscious and unconscious, transcends the powers of imagination. We can easily conceive of a part of this totality as our persona, but we struggle unsuccessfully to comprehend our whole. The self remains a "superordinate quantity" (Jung, 1958, p. 127).

Whatever its appellation and wherever its residence in our consciousness, located specifically or diffused throughout our entire span of inner and outer consciousness, we, as therapists, can help clients access this personal inborn healing system.

❖ *Meditation*

The oldest major source of theory and practice underlying Meditative Therapy is meditation — most specifically mindfulness meditation methods. In ancient times, long before the advent of psychotherapy, meditative practices provided a complete system of inner mind exploration and healing. The *Vissudhimaga*, a Buddhist text from the fifth century A.D., gives comprehensive information on one viewpoint of meditation; methods of training attention, states of consciousness, and psychological consequences of experiencing these states. It categorizes meditation into two approaches: meditative concentration and mindfulness insight. Psychologist Daniel Goleman (1977) describes the methods utilized in each approach in *The Varieties of the Meditative Experience.*

Concentrative Meditation. In meditative concentration, Goleman (1977) explains that attention is focused onto a single object. The *Vissudhimaga* cites forty objects (e.g., a flower, a tree) of concentration. These objects can be viewed externally or pictured internally. This process, termed "one pointed concentration," emphasizes the continual return to one point of concentration each time the mind wanders. By repeatedly refocusing on one point of concentration, the meditator gains control of the mind.

Mindfulness Meditation. The second category of the *Vissudhimaga*, "the path of insight," is based on mindfulness. Mindfulness differs from concentrative meditation in its focus. In mindfulness meditation, the meditator passively observes the workings of the mind, rather than a single point of concentration, such as an image or word. Nyanaponika Thera, a modern Buddhist monk, describes mindfulness as "the clear and single-minded awareness of what actually happens to us and in us, at the successive moments of perception" (Goleman, 1977, p. 22).

In observing the workings of the mind, the meditator can center on the body, the feelings, the mind, or on mind objects. In mindfulness of the body, the meditator notices each instant of bodily response, such as movements or positions. Mindfulness of feelings focuses on inner sensations regardless of their content. Feelings can be pleasant or unpleasant, but the meditator continues in spite of the valence of the feelings. In mindfulness of mental states, the meditator centers on moods, thoughts, or psychological states as each occurs. Mindfulness of mind objects closely resembles mindfulness of mental states. Yet, in addition, the meditator categorizes these mind objects as either furthering or blocking the path to enlightenment.

Usually, training in concentrative methods is recommended prior to practicing mindfulness meditation. However, the meditator may also use "bare insight." In bare insight, the meditator begins mindfulness without prior training and concentration develops through the practice of mindfulness itself. A certain level of concentration is necessary to sustain self-observation. With practice, the meditator notices every movement of the mind without break. In this manner, the practice of mindfulness develops a dual consciousness: the "observing I" watches what we think of as the "I" that thinks, feels, and acts (Goleman, 1977, p. 98).

The practice of mindfulness meditation leads to three important realizations about the nature of mind: 1. It is "not self"; 2. It is impermanent; 3. It is the source of suffering. At the peak of detachment from mental phenomena, a consciousness of "Nirvana," a realm beyond known reality, arises. This experience leads to significant changes in the meditator's consciousness. George Gurdjieff (1877-1949), a twentieth century mystic, describes these changes in terms more easily accepted and understood by the western mind. By reaching objective consciousness, the meditator is liberated from "arbitrary, irrational influences from internal and external sources, respectively" (Goleman, 1977, p. 101).

Mindfulness Meditation and Psychological Treatment. Since 1979, psychologist Jon Kabat-Zinn (1982) has administered a chronic pain, stress reduction, and relaxation program at the University of Massachusetts Medical Center in Worcester. Mindfulness meditation is the key component of the program, which consists of eight weekly two-hour sessions. Two therapists meet with up to thirty clients during these sessions. In addition, participants complete daily homework exercises.

Research studies on the Kabat-Zinn mindfulness meditation program document a number of important outcomes: decreases in physical and psychological symptoms, Astin (1997); Hellman, et al. (1990); Tate (1994); decreases in physical pain among chronic pain patients, Kabat-Zinn and others (1982); (1985); (1987); reduction in anxiety levels, Kabat-Zinn (1992); Boswell and Murray (1979); Miller, et al. (1993), improvement in psoriasis, Bernhard & Kabat-Zinn (1988); and decreased symptoms of fibromyalgia, Kaplan, et al. (1993).

Kabat-Zinn's fame grew after he was featured on the public television series "Healing and the Mind" hosted by Bill Moyers in 1993. A transcript of the series was published in a book of the same title (Moyers, 1993). Partly as a result of that program, over one-hundred health care settings now offer mindfulness-based stress reduction programs. Through meditation, patients with chronic medical and mental health problems are taught to improve their health and the quality of their lives.

One such clinic, The Stress Reduction and Relaxation Clinic at the Community Health Center in Meriden, Connecticut, is headed by Beth Roth, a family and pediatric practitioner. According to Roth (1997), Kabat-Zinn's mindfulness meditation approach begins with training in concentrative meditation. The focal point or point of concentration is one's breathing. The physical sensations of breathing such as the flow of air in and out of the nostrils, or the rise and fall of the chest and abdomen provide the focus of attention. When attention wanders off into thoughts or memories, the participant gently returns attention to breathing. This process of concentrative meditation develops the skill of moment-to-moment awareness.

As the meditator progresses in the ability to concentrate, mindfulness practice may begin. The meditator: "observes the constant stream of thoughts, emotions, and body sensations that comprises one's life experience" (Roth, 1967, p. 53). This is done without preferring any experience over another, by refraining from judgment, comment, elaboration, censorship, interpretation, and emotional reaction.

Teasdale, et al. (1995), elaborate further, stating that the essence of the mindfulness state taught by Kabat-Zinn is: "to 'be' fully in the present moment, without judging or evaluating it, without reflecting backwards on past memories, without looking forward to anticipate the future, as in anxious worry, and without attempting to 'problem-solve' or otherwise avoid any unpleasant aspects of the immediate situation" (Teasdale, 1995, p. 33).

The mindful state, according to Teasdale, avoids elaborate, ruminative thinking about one's situation and its origins, implications and associations. This reduces the tendency to "float away" into elaborate thought streams. This statement implies that the participant in mindfulness meditation would not allow deeper level psychological material to unfold. However, research into this topic points out the potential for such occurrences.

Depth Possibilities with Mindfulness. John Miller, M.D. (1993), describes mindfulness meditation as "developing a spotlight quality of consciousness, whereby any passing mind-object can become the object of the mind's attention." The intent is to deepen self-understanding, which leads toward overcoming suffering. The meditator's attitude toward mind objects remains calm, neutral, free of self-involvement, and judgment about what takes place.

In his article, "The unveiling of traumatic memories and emotions through mindfulness and concentration meditation: Clinical implications and three case reports," Miller agrees that mindfulness meditation (MM) often "reduces stress, fear, anxiety, and dysphoria" (Miller, 1993, p. 170). However, he cautions that painful or repressed psychological material may arise during MM. He presents three case studies of individuals who had reactions of this nature during intensive MM retreats. All three individuals had experienced physical and/or sexual abuse in the past. The meditation experience eventually became very intense for these three individuals and all were subsequently placed on medication and received psychotherapy.

These examples point to the power of MM to uncover past trauma and intense emotions. They also demonstrate the need for adequate screening guidelines, informed consent, knowledge of the complete range of possible reaction to inner work, and an understanding of the Meditative Therapy therapeutic approach.

It's important to have a complete understanding of the range of depth and power the Inner Source possesses in helping a client or a mindfulness meditation practitioner. This knowledge can prepare the meditation teacher or psychotherapist to recognize, support and guide the meditator's reaction to experiencing a deeper level psychological, physical, or spiritual experience.

At the same time, it's important to realize that meditation-based approaches are different than a psychotherapy approach like Meditative Therapy.

Relationship Between Meditation and Meditative Therapy. Mindfulness meditation contributes several key aspects to MT, most notably, the process of passively observing inner mental processes. It also describes the states of altered consciousness and psychological benefits derived from such experiences. Meditative Therapy experiences may resemble experiences of mindfulness meditators. However, since MT occurs within a psychological setting, rather than a religious setting, important differences are apparent.

Two main factors help differentiate meditation from Meditative Therapy: The *process* factor and the *purpose* factor.

The Process Factor. The process of concentrative or mindfulness meditation and meditative therapy is very similar. All of these methods results in an inner flow of experiences, which unfolds psychological, physiological, and spiritual material. However, three main differences in process point to the psychotherapeutic nature of Meditative Therapy: time and depth, verbalization, and the presence of a therapist.

Meditative Therapy is purposefully set up to be psycho-therapeutic in nature and the *amount of time allowed* is an important aspect of that purpose. In MM and CM, the meditation session is usually restricted to thirty minutes, or twenty minutes twice a day. In Meditative Therapy, the Inner Source ideally designates how much time an MT session should last. The amount of time is not pre-set and sessions may last from thirty minutes to ninety minutes. Initially, most sessions seem to end naturally within sixty to ninety minutes. As the Inner Source processes the material, the amount of time needed often levels out at forty-five to sixty minutes.

The increased amount of time permitted in MT allows a greater *depth of response*. Recall the many examples of therapeutic experiences given in Chapter 5. Abreactions and extended discharging illustrate a depth that wouldn't be allowed to develop in a time-limited meditation approach. It is difficult to imagine interrupting an abreaction sequence regularly to return to a point of concentration or to automatically arise after fifteen, twenty, or thirty minutes due to a pre-set finishing time. Inner Source processing must be allowed adequate time to reach its depth potential.

A time-honored tradition in psychotherapy acknowledges the healing power of verbalization. The term "the talking cure" emphasizes the value of processing psychological difficulties out loud. Descriptions of the concentrative meditation and advanced mindfulness insight meditation approaches do not mention describing inner material aloud. In Meditative Therapy, one of the essential requirements is for the participant to report orally everything that takes place.

Statements said out loud either lose power or gain power on a much deeper level than when they are kept inside. Spoken words appear to have a healing effect. Because they are out in the open, not hidden, words take on new meaning. One client recognized this during her first Meditative Therapy session, "Boy, when you speak out loud, the words are bigger than the thoughts. Words make thoughts seem really silly."

Words also make thoughts seem wise. Words said out loud can provide positive reinforcement. An example would be, "I feel good about myself. I am feeling a lot more self-confident." How many of us say this out loud to ourselves even with our eyes open? Seldom do we even allow ourselves to think it. When the Inner Source prompts us to realize certain positive insights and we state these insights out loud, they take on a new power.

The final difference in process has to do with the *presence of a therapist*. Meditation frequently occurs in solitude or in groups of meditators. Outside of teaching situations, the meditator rarely meditates with an individual guide. Due to the potential depth of response that can instantly develop in MT, a caring and knowledgeable therapist must be present. The therapist acts as an anchor during intense, overwhelming, confusing or unwieldy abreactive sequences. At such times, the therapist's reassuring presence enables the client to stay with the process. One client expressed the importance of the therapist's presence by saying, "You were right there with me, I felt the connection. We were sharing this at a very deep level."

The Purpose Factor.   Perhaps the most important difference between meditation and Meditative Therapy deals with purpose. Meditative Therapy is designed to be a psychotherapy, whereas meditation approaches are not. This statement does not deny the well-documented psychological benefit of meditation, but only that meditation's purpose is not deep psychological change.

Due to MT's purpose, the meditative material is dealt with in a manner consistent with psychotherapy. While the MT experience is in and of itself healing for the client, it also contributes greatly to the overall process of therapy. Transcripts are read and re-read and the material serves as a basis for exploration, interpretation, and integration.

While recording and tracking the MT experience, the therapist gains valuable insight into the client's history, destructive cognitive and behavioral patterns, physical problems, spiritual issues, strengths, and unresolved issues (such as losses and traumatic experiences). Frequently, metaphoric images and themes emerge that inform future sessions. Often the MT material helps the clinician select needed adjuncts to therapy such as assertiveness training or anger management. Finally, MT sessions can also help therapists track client progress; sessions become shorter and less intense, for example, as clients improve.

❖ *Spiritual Traditions*

Ralph Waldo Emerson acknowledged the timelessness of great ideas when he said, "All my best thoughts were stolen by the ancients." Indeed, a multitude of ancient eastern and western spiritual teachers have contributed valuable wisdom to Meditative Therapy. Four ideas deserve special consideration: the *oneness of God*, the *inner availability of the experience of oneness*, the *symbolism of light*, and the *realization of enlightenment*.

The sages of all sacred traditions agree on the oneness that pervades the multiplicity and duality of the universe. The *handogya Upanishad* describes Brahman — absolute reality — as "One without a second" (White, 1973). From the western perspective, Isaiah echoes this truth as "I am the Lord, and there is none else."

Both Eastern and Western spiritual traditions teach that we are spiritual beings, emanations of this oneness, as well as bodies and minds. Paul Brunton, writing from the perspective of traditional Yoga, terms our spiritual nature "the Overself." He describes the Overself as "the ray of God in man, the source of all enduring bliss, divine consciousness, man's essential being, fadeless, earthless, ageless, timeless, unlimited, and the innermost living core" (Brunton 1937). Zen Buddhism agrees that truth and wisdom are available within each person. In *The Three Pillars of Zen*, Kapleau (1967) describes the Bodhi-mind as "the innate dignity of man," "the vibrant awareness of living Truth," "intrinsic wisdom" and the "reverse of the mind of delusion and ignorance." Western mystical writers also speak of the God-within. Ralph Waldo Emerson stated that "God is here within." He elaborates on this belief in his description of the Over-soul: "Meantime within man is the soul of the whole; the wise silence, the universal beauty, to which every part and particle is equally related; the eternal One" (Atkinson, p. 263).

Many sacred teachings use light to symbolize the divine. The word *enlightenment* refers to the realization of "the truth of Being. Our native condition, our true self is Being, traditionally called God, the Cosmic Person, the Supreme Being, the One-in-all." Thus the very word enlightenment alludes to God as light. "No other words seem quite as revealing of the mystical experience as those related to light: illumination, enlightenment, inner light, vision, radiant, burning, shining, dazzling, bright" (Embler, 1974).

White (1972) states that according to Aldous Huxley, the light experience is central to spiritual experiences and is often described in the Bible and other religious literature. In John 8, for example, Jesus says, "I am the light of the world: he that followeth me shall not walk in darkness, but shall have the light of life." In *The Bhagavad Gita*, Krishna also speaks of God as light:

> *He who finds his joy within*
> *Within, his grove of pleasure*
> *And the light of the sun within,*
> *Merging with God, he gains God's bliss.*
> (Stanford, 1970, p. 45)

Carl Jung, in his commentary on *The Secret of the Golden Flower*, an ancient Chinese text on meditation, speaks of the effects of the light experience:

> *Its effect is astonishing in that it almost always brings*
> *about a solution of psychic complications, and thereby frees the*
> *inner personality from emotional and intellectual*
> *entanglements, creating thus a unity of being which is*
> *universally felt as "liberation."* (Wilhelm, 1962, p. 107)

Liberation is another word for enlightenment, the freedom that results from the realization of the truth of Being. Buddha characterized enlightenment as the absence of hatred, greed, and ignorance. Theravadin Buddhism, the oldest Buddhist teachings which date back almost 2,000 years, describes ten traits or "perfections" that characterize a fully enlightened person. The cultivation of the "ten perfections" is process oriented. All humans possess these traits in varying degrees and can enhance these qualities by leading an ethical life style, meditating and developing wisdom. The "ten perfections" include: determination, energy, ethicality, truthfulness, renunciation, patience, equanimity, generosity, loving kindness, and wisdom. Although not an exhaustive list, these qualities are valued by all the great spiritual disciplines (White, 1972, p. 141).

The four spiritual concepts discussed in this section are not foreign to the field of psychology: Carl Jung, Eric Fromm,

Abraham Maslow, Lawrence Kohlberg, and Ken Wilber have acknowledged similar ideas. These spiritual concepts could also be expressed in psychological terms. However, exploring MT's spiritual roots acknowledges the inherent spiritual quality to the Meditative Therapy process. Experiences of the oneness of the universe, the inner connection to oneness, light, and enlightenment abound in Meditative Therapy. Allowing, trusting, and validating these experiences allows the full beauty and power of Meditative Therapy to unfold.

Although we personally believe that the Inner Source is inherently spiritual or divine, Meditative Therapy works regardless of belief systems. From a practical psychotherapeutic viewpoint, the term *Inner Source* avoids a blatantly spiritual connotation. This neutral term avoids forcing a spiritual position onto therapists or clients. A skillful therapist speaks in a language the client can hear and understand. The therapist may choose to speak of the holographic model of brain processing, the psychological model of personal growth or the spiritual model of the process of enlightenment. Regardless of terminology, Meditative Therapy liberates clients from psychological dysfunction and moves them towards integration and well being. Through this method, the paths of the spiritual journey and the therapeutic process converge.

Four psychotherapies, together with concepts of a higher consciousness, provide a theoretical and scientific basis for Meditative Therapy. When joined with ancient spiritual traditions and meditation practices, they form the roots of Meditative Therapy. Meditative Therapy continues in the tradition of eyes-closed, inner-oriented psychotherapy, but seeks to restore the spiritual essence of this self-healing process.

14 ❖

Ten Important Points About Meditative Therapy

1. Meditative Therapy is an inner-directed, therapeutic approach which facilitates a natural altered state of consciousness, allowing the client's Inner Source to engage in a holistic self-unifying and self-healing process.

2. Meditative Therapy is a psycho-spiritual approach, which draws from time-honored traditions of mindfulness meditation, inner-oriented psychotherapy, consciousness, and spirituality.

3. Holographic brain theory, which proposes that information scattered throughout the brain is connected by paths traversed by light, provides a basis for understanding the nature of Inner Source processing. Explicate and implicate reality connect, to display whatever the client needs for healing and growth, through MT sequences imaged by the brain.

4. The Inner Source process is timeless (containing past, present and future), allows for rapid healing and learning, and can display unusual phenomena such as bright light and out-of-body experiences.

5. The Inner Source works holistically — with the client's mind, body, and spirit — to achieve healing and creative goals that lead to new dimensions of integration and growth.

6. The Inner Source process is naturally integrative and makes use of methods from many theoretical orientations in order to achieve therapeutic and creative goals for the client.

7. There is minimal need for the therapist or client to direct or interpret the Inner Source material during Meditative Therapy. Post-session, client-centered interpretive techniques may, however, further client insight and integration of the experience.

8. Therapist preparation to utilize MT includes appropriate psychotherapy credentials, previous training in inner-oriented psychotherapies, familiarity with meditative and spiritual disciplines, and training in MT (through reading *Meditative Therapy* and/or attending MT workshops).

9. Appropriate client selection, education regarding the process of MT, and informed consent provide important safeguards for the application of Meditative Therapy.

10. Qualitative research has demonstrated the effectiveness of MT. Most participants stated that MT created lasting benefits and a resolution of presenting problems. Forty percent regarded MT as "the greatest thing that ever happened" to them.

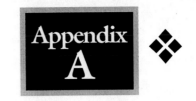

Sample Fear Inventory Items [1]

The Fear Inventory or Fear Survey Schedule (FSS) is a self-report test wherein one can rate the degree to which various things and experiences cause a fearful or unpleasant reaction. Four sample items are given below:

	Not At All	A Little	A Fair Amount	Much	Very Much
1. Enclosed places	|_____	_____	_____	_____	_____|
2. Failure	|_____	_____	_____	_____	_____|
3. Being Teased	|_____	_____	_____	_____	_____|
4. Feeling Disapproved of	|_____	_____	_____	_____	_____|

The particular FSS which I administered to my clients contained 76 items. There is a much more thorough FSS which contain 122 items, and is available to professionals through the Educational and Industrial Testing Services, (EDITS), P.O. Box 7234, San Diego, CA 92107.

The scoring system which I utilized on the 76 item FSS was to give a 1 for Not at All; 2 for A Little; 2 for A Fair Amount; 4 for Much; 5 for Very Much. The total possible score was 380.

---

1 Sample items from the Fear Survey Schedule, Copyright 1969 by Educational and Industrial Testing Service. All rights reserved. Reproduced with permission.

Willoughby Personality Schedule[1]

Instructions: the questions in this schedule are intended to indicate various emotional personality traits. It is not a test in any sense because there are no right and wrong answers to any of the questions in this schedule.

After each question you will find a row of numbers whose meaning is given below. All you have to do is to draw a circle around the number that describes you best.

0 means "no," "never," "not at all," etc.
1 means "somewhat," "sometimes," "a little," etc.
2 means "about as often as not," "an average amount," etc.
3 means "usually," "a good deal," "rather often," etc.
4 means "practically always," "entirely," etc.

1. Do you get stage fright?	0 1 2 3 4
2. Do you worry over humiliating experiences?	0 1 2 3 4
3. Are you afraid of falling when you are on a high place?	0 1 2 3 4
4. Are your feelings easily hurt?	0 1 2 3 4
5. Do you keep in the background on social occasions?	0 1 2 3 4
6. Are you happy and sad by turns without knowing why?	0 1 2 3 4
7. Are you shy?	0 1 2 3 4
8. Do you day-dream frequently?	0 1 2 3 4
9. Do you get discouraged easily?	0 1 2 3 4
10. Do you say things on the spur of the moment and then regret them?	0 1 2 3 4

1 From Wolpe, J. *The Practice of Behavior Therapy* (Second Edition). Elmsford, N. Y.: Pergamon Press, 1973. A short form of the Clark-Thurstone Inventory, known as "Willoughby's Neuroticism Schedule." See Willoughby, R.R., "Norms for the Clark-Thurstone Inventory," *Journal of Social Psychology,* 5: 91, 1934. Reproduced by permission of Joseph Wolpe.

11. Do you like to be alone?   0 1 2 3 4

12. Do you cry easily?   0 1 2 3 4

13. Does it bother you to have people watch you work
    even when you do it well?   0 1 2 3 4

14. Does criticism hurt you badly?   0 1 2 3 4

15. Do you cross the street to avoid meeting someone?   0 1 2 3 4

16. At a reception or tea do you avoid meeting the
    important person present?   0 1 2 3 4

17. Do you often feel just miserable?   0 1 2 3 4

18. Do you hesitate to volunteer in a class discussion
    or debate?   0 1 2 3 4

19. Are you often lonely?   0 1 2 3 4

20. Are you self-conscious before superiors?   0 1 2 3 4

21. Do you lack self-confidence?   0 1 2 3 4

22. Are you self-conscious about your appearance?   0 1 2 3 4

23. If you see an accident does something keep you
    from giving help?   0 1 2 3 4

24. Do you feel inferior?   0 1 2 3 4

25. Is it hard to make up your mind until the time
    for action is past?   0 1 2 3 4

Follow-Up of Counseling Form

P lease complete the following individualized evaluation of counseling form. Your feelings about your experience are extremely important to me. I need the feedback in order to have information concerning the usefulness of the various approaches which I employ. Also, I feel it would be good for you to evaluate your own progress.

After completing the form, place it in the envelope provided, seal it, and then return it to the secretary who will make sure I receive the material.

Sincerely,

Michael L. Emmons, Ph.D.
Counseling Psychologist

When you came to us for counseling in _____, you indicated that your difficulties were as follows:

A.   J.

B.
                                    K.
C.

D.   L.

E.

F.   M.

G.
                                    N.
H.

I.   O.

1. Please rate the degree to which these difficulties changed on the following scales. Use the A. scale for the A. difficulty listed above, the B. scale for the B. difficulty listed above and so on.

A.

Total Improvement	Very Much Improved	Much Improved	Average Improvement	Somewhat Improved	Slight Improvement	No Improvement

B.

Total Improvement	Very Much Improved	Much Improved	Average Improvement	Somewhat Improved	Slight Improvement	No Improvement

C.

Total Improvement	Very Much Improved	Much Improved	Average Improvement	Somewhat Improved	Slight Improvement	No Improvement

D.

Total Improvement	Very Much Improved	Much Improved	Average Improvement	Somewhat Improved	Slight Improvement	No Improvement

E.

Total Improvement	Very Much Improved	Much Improved	Average Improvement	Somewhat Improved	Slight Improvement	No Improvement

F.

Total Improvement	Very Much Improved	Much Improved	Average Improvement	Somewhat Improved	Slight Improvement	No Improvement

G.

Total Improvement	Very Much Improved	Much Improved	Average Improvement	Somewhat Improved	Slight Improvement	No Improvement

H.

Total Improvement	Very Much Improved	Much Improved	Average Improvement	Somewhat Improved	Slight Improvement	No Improvement

I.

Total Improvement	Very Much Improved	Much Improved	Average Improvement	Somewhat Improved	Slight Improvement	No Improvement

J.

Total Improvement	Very Much Improved	Much Improved	Average Improvement	Somewhat Improved	Slight Improvement	No Improvement

K.

Total Improvement	Very Much Improved	Much Improved	Average Improvement	Somewhat Improved	Slight Improvement	No Improvement

L.

Total Improvement	Very Much Improved	Much Improved	Average Improvement	Somewhat Improved	Slight Improvement	No Improvement

M.

Total Improvement	Very Much Improved	Much Improved	Average Improvement	Somewhat Improved	Slight Improvement	No Improvement

N.

Total Improvement	Very Much Improved	Much Improved	Average Improvement	Somewhat Improved	Slight Improvement	No Improvement

O.

Total Improvement	Very Much Improved	Much Improved	Average Improvement	Somewhat Improved	Slight Improvement	No Improvement

2. Please indicate in the space provided other changes, positive and negative, you've observed since beginning your counseling experience.

3. Answer the questions listed below only if they are check-marked with red.
   A. Do you feel you benefited from Assertiveness Training?
      Yes, No (circle one).
   B. Do you feel you benefited from dietary suggestions and changes in your diet?
      Yes, No (circle one). Please give specific reasons for your answer.
   C. Do you feel you benefited from Meditative Therapy?
      Yes, No (circle one). Please give specific reasons for your answer.
   D. Do you feel you benefited from regular talk therapy?
      Yes, No (circle one). Please give specific reasons for your answer.
   E. Do you feel you benefited from systematic desensitization?
      Yes, No (circle one). Please give specific reasons for your answer.
   F. Do you feel you benefited from the use of the video tape recorder?
      Yes, No (circle). Please give specific reasons for your answer.
   G. Do you feel you benefited from marital counseling sessions with your spouse?
      Yes, No (circle one). Please give specific reasons for your answer.

4. Which of the above therapies do you feel was the most beneficial to you?

5. What was the most outstanding factor in your counseling experience?

6. How might I improve my approach so as to be more helpful to future clients?

7. Have any other events taken place in your life during the counseling period that might account for the changes you have noted?

Meditative Therapy
Follow-Up Questionnaire

Please complete the following questionnaire concerning your feelings about your experiences with Meditative Therapy (closing your eyes and allowing an inner intelligence or higher self to help you). Keep in mind that you are not expected to answer in one way or another, that there are no right or wrong answers. I am only interested in hearing your honest evaluation of your experiences.

Sincerely,

Michael Emmons

Rate the following remarks on the scale provided:
   0 means "not at all"   2 means "quite a bit"
   1 means "a little"   3 means "very much"

1. Looking back on your Meditative Therapy experiences, how would you rate the experience as a whole?

A very pleasant experience	0	1	2	3
Something I want to try again	0	1	2	3
An experience of great beauty	0	1	2	3
Greater awareness of reality	0	1	2	3
Feel it was of lasting benefit to me	0	1	2	3
The greatest thing that ever happened to me	0	1	2	3
A religious experience	0	1	2	3
A very unpleasant experience	0	1	2	3
A disappointing experience	0	1	2	3
An experience of insanity	0	1	2	3
Did me harm mentally	0	1	2	3

Like traveling to a far-off land   0 1 2 3
Very much like being drunk   0 1 2 3
Return to feelings of childhood   0 1 2 3
Physical discomfort and illness   0 1 2 3

2. How were you, or what were you left with, after your Meditative Therapy experiences?

A new way of looking at the world   0 1 2 3

A greater understanding of the importance and
meaning of human relationships   0 1 2 3

A new understanding of beauty and art   0 1 2 3

A greater awareness of God, or a Higher Power,
or an Ultimate Reality   0 1 2 3

A sense of greater regard for the welfare and
comfort of other human beings   0 1 2 3

More ability to relax and be myself   0 1 2 3

Improvement noted by people closest to me   0 1 2 3

Greater tolerance of others   0 1 2 3

A sense of futility and emptiness   0 1 2 3

A frightening feeling that I might go crazy or
lose control of myself   0 1 2 3

Sense of relaxation and freedom from anxiety and tension   0 1 2 3

A better understanding of the cause and source of
my troubles   0 1 2 3

A set of new decisions and new directions for my life   0 1 2 3

A new sense of fun and enjoyment   0 1 2 3

A sense of now knowing what life is all about   0 1 2 3

Colors have been brighter   0 1 2 3

3. Have you taken psychedelic drugs of any kind prior to your Meditative Therapy experiences?
Circle: Yes   No
If yes, please list them and explain under what conditions you took them.

4. How would you compare the two experiences? Any similarities, etc.?

5. What was your involvement in religion as you were growing up? Please explain.

6. How would you describe your involvement with religious or spiritual matters as an adult prior to your Meditative Therapy experiences?

7. Have your feelings on religion and what it means changed any as a result of your Meditative Therapy experiences?
Circle: Yes   No
If yes, in what way?

8. Have your experiences with Meditative Therapy changed your feelings about death in any way?
Circle: Yes   No
If yes, explain:

9. Do you trust God or a supreme being or concept more than you did? How?
Circle: Yes   No

10. Have your ideas concerning parapsychological experiences such ESP, out-of-body experiences, etc., changed as a result of your Meditative Therapy experiences?
Circle: Yes   No
If yes, explain:

11. Please explain what role I, as the therapist, played in your Meditative Therapy experiences.

12. Is there anything else you can tell of your experiences that was particularly exciting, disturbing, unusual, etc.? Please share it with me.

What Clients Want to Know About Meditative Therapy

The following questions and answers are designed to give you an overview of Meditative Therapy. Most people wonder about these questions prior to experiencing MT.

Q: *What is Meditative Therapy?*
A: Meditative Therapy (MT) is an inner-oriented process directed by your Inner Source. The Inner Source is an aspect of higher consciousness that facilitates self-healing. Many names have been used to refer to this in-born, self-healing capacity. Some names stress the spiritual nature of this source, such as *Higher Self, Buddha Nature,* and *God Within.* Other names point to a physiological basis, like *brain-directed process* and *information processing system.* MT works, regardless of what we call it.

Q: *What will I do during Meditative Therapy?*
A: You'll sit or lie down, close your eyes, and concentrate inwardly with the conscious intention of receiving help. Then you will describe out loud anything that comes into your awareness. You may notice a variety of holistic sensations such as physical reactions (feeling hot, cold, tense, etc.), thoughts, feelings and/or visual images (colors, light, people, places, objects, etc.). The idea is to watch passively, without judging or resisting what you see or experience. As you focus inwardly, you will enter an altered state of consciousness and begin your own therapeutic journey, guided by your personal Inner Source.

Q: *What is it like to be in this altered state of consciousness?*
A: The state is similar to that experienced in mindfulness meditation. Although you'll remain aware of your surroundings, you'll focus primarily on your "inner screen." This allows an inner flow of experiences to unfold, involving your body, mind and spirit. Although the experience can feel "deep," you'll remain in charge and can choose to stop if you wish. However, it's best to allow the process to end naturally. The Inner Source may signal an ending by giving you an image, such as a book closing, or a feeling that it's over, or you may simply stop receiving additional material. Afterward, you may notice that the time spent in MT seems very short, when actually it may have taken sixty to ninety minutes. It may take you a few minutes to reorient to your surroundings.

Q: *What types of experiences might I encounter on this journey?*
A: It's difficult to predict exactly what any one person will experience. Your Inner Source generates whatever material that is needed for your healing and growth. In general, you'll have two types of experiences: *therapeutic* and *creative*. Therapeutic experiences involve dealing with problem areas such as past disturbing or traumatic events. You may re-experience traumatic events that have remained unresolved, such as a serious illness or the death of a loved one. This may involve emotional or physical discomfort as discharging occurs. However, the relief resulting from staying with the process usually makes most clients feel that the gain was worth the pain. Creative experiences may involve unusual sensations such as spinning, seeing light, or experiencing variety of parapsychological events. These experiences seem to foster growth.

Q: *What does the therapist do during Meditative Therapy?*
A: Your therapist will be present at all times and help you enter the Inner Source process and stay with it until it ends. The therapist will talk to you as needed, offering directions or encouragement. The therapist will also keep track of the time and help you end if the session goes over the allotted time. After the session, the therapist will de-brief the experience with you and make sure that

you're aware, alert and ready to leave the office. The therapist will also remain available during the week, if needed.

Q: *What should I do between sessions?*
A: The therapist will give you a written transcript of your session to read several times during the week. You may continue to experience feelings, thoughts, images etc. that relate to your session as you re-read your transcript. Sometimes dreams or past memories occur. This is a normal part of the MT experience. Notice whatever comes up and write it down, so that you can report back to your therapist. If you experience a high level of physical or emotional disturbance which doesn't resolve, call your therapist. Your therapist may be able to help you resolve this disturbance over the phone or you may need to schedule an appointment.

If you have any other questions regarding MT, please ask your therapist. Any concerns that go unaddressed may prevent you from fully entering into MT. Usually, once you discuss your concerns, you'll be able to proceed.

It's hard to predict whether you will like or benefit from MT. Most clients report a significant reduction in their symptoms within five to ten sessions, but no two clients are exactly alike. The best way to find out is to experience one or two sessions. In a group of forty-two clients, forty percent viewed MT as "the greatest thing that ever happened" to them.

Consent for Meditative Therapy Treatment

I have been informed that Meditative Therapy (MT) is a relatively unknown treatment approach which has not been widely validated by research.

I have been advised that MT is a holistically oriented therapy which deals with mental, physical and spiritual reaction and content. In addition, I have been informed that the MT process may provoke unusual or intense physical, psychological or spiritual reactions. In addition, I have been notified of the possibility of having abreactive or cathartic experiences, usually based on past painful or traumatic events in my life. Theses reactions might include physical pain, fear, crying, nightmares, and flashbacks and are known to be curative in nature, but may be upsetting.

I understand the nature of MT and the possibility of upsetting reactions and hereby give my consent to receive Meditative Therapy treatment. My signature is being given voluntarily, free from pressure from any person.

Client Signature_____

Date_____

Appendix G ❖

Creating Safety and Closure

P rior to beginning Meditative Therapy, the therapist should be familiar with the following three exercises that can help clients return to a sense of safety and calm, when they feel overwhelmed or threatened by disturbing material, either during or outside of a session.

1. The Safe Space Exercise
Although this exercise is widely used, we first encountered it in *Eye Movement Desensitization and Reprocessing* (Shapiro, 1995). Shapiro credits this exercise to Miller (1994), whose tape "Letting Go of Stress," provides an excellent guided visualization to creating a safe place.

In the Safe Space Exercise, the client creates an inner haven which is available by merely closing the eyes and visualizing this place.

Step 1 Ask the client to imagine a place which evokes a sense of safety, well-being and calm. This may be a real or imaginary location. Perhaps the scene that comes to mind will be an ocean shore, a wooded scene, or a familiar room. Frequently clients choose places from childhood that are associated with pleasant memories.

Step 2 Ask the client to describe the place using sensory details, such as smells, tactile sensations, sounds, and sight.

Step 3 Ask the client to describe the emotions and physical sensations that accompany being at the safe place.

Step 4 Ask the client to create a short phrase to access the safe place, such as "my cottage at the beach," "thatched roof," or "ocean air."

Step 5 Practice using the safe place during the session by asking the client to imagine an irritating situation, like waiting in a long line or being stuck in a traffic jam. Assess the level of disturbance from 1-10 (1=low disturbance and 10=high disturbance). For practice, a 5 level of disturbance works well. Ask the client to imagine the safe place and focus on this scene until feeling more relaxed. Then reassess the level of disturbance. In most cases, the client will report feeling more relaxed, with the disturbance level decreased to possible a 3 or 2. This can be repeated several times.

Step 6 Instruct clients to practice the safe place visualization at home several times per week, using the key phrase to access the scene.

Clinicians trained in EMDR may wish to follow Shapiro's instructions for creating a safe place found on page 122 of *Eye Movement Densensitization and Reprocessing* (Shapiro, 1995).

2. The Light-Stream Exercise
We first encountered a variation of this technique at a meditation retreat in 1988. Shapiro (1995) explains that her exercise is based on a yoga exercise used by Levine, author of *Guided Meditation* (1991), to alleviate chronic pain. In this exercise, the client uses a colored light to heal emotional disturbance located in an area of the body.

As Shapiro explains, prior to using the technique, the clinician must check out the client's ability to identify body sensations that accompany a moderately disturbing scene, such as taking a test. Ask the client to mentally scan his or her body and notice how it feels. Next ask the client to imagine a moderately disturbing scene and then notice the resulting changes in his or her body. Once the client can identify bodily sensations that accompany a disturbing scene, the therapist can proceed with the Light-Stream Exercise.

Step 1 Ask the client to concentrate on body sensations: "Where do you feel the disturbance in your body?" The client responds by naming the chest, stomach, throat, etc.

Step 2 Ask the client to give the feeling a shape: "If the feeling had a shape, what shape would it be?" The client responds by describing the shape as round, square, triangular, etc.

Step 3 Ask the client to give the feeling a color: "If the feeling had a color, what color would it be?" The client responds by naming the color as black, red, etc.

Step 4 Ask the client to give the feeling a size: "If the feeling had a size, how large would it be?" The client responds by describing the size.

Step 5 Ask the client to name a color that would be healing. Any color, except the same color for the disturbing feeling, may be used: "What color would be healing for this disturbing feeling?"

Step 6 Ask the client to imagine the following:
"See the healing light enter through the top of your head and flow toward the disturbing shape (name the shape). Since the source of the lights is the Universe, as much light as you need is available. Imagine the light surrounding and interacting with the shape... more and more light... healing. Just watch. Don't force it. Just allow the light to work."

Then check with the client for feedback.
"Can you see that?" "What's happening now?"
If the client reports a change in color, shape or size, etc., the therapist repeats a version of Step 6, until the shape disappears, becomes transparent, or transforms. (If no change happens, another exercise should be used.) Usually, the transformation of the shape accompanies a decrease in disturbance.

Step 7 Once the client reports that the disturbing feeling has decreased, the therapist can continue as follows:
"As the light enters the top of your head, allow it to fill up your entire head. Now see it flow down your neck,

into your shoulders and down your arms and into you
hands and out your fingertips. Now see it following
from your neck into your chest, your abdomen, hips,
legs, and out the bottom of your feet."

When the client looks relaxed, give the suggestion that the
peaceful, relaxed feeling can be brought back and retained
throughout the week. Ask the client to become awake and
aware by the (slow) count of five.

3. Putting Away the Disturbance
In this exercise, the therapist leads the client through the Light
Stream Exercise up to Step 7. After completing Step 6, if the
client reports that a part of the shape remains accompanied by a
moderate level of disturbance, the therapist may ask the client if
she/he would like to put away the disturbance until the next
session. If the client chooses to put it away, the therapist follows
these steps:
1. Imagine that you can reach in, remove the shape and put in a
safe place, until our next session. If you'd like, you can leave it
in my office, in the filing cabinet or my desk. Perhaps you have
a safe place at home, a chest, a safe, etc.
2. See yourself put the shape in whatever place you've chosen.
3. Remember that you will come back and deal with this matter
next week. You don't have to carry it around all week.
4. When you've completed the task, open your eyes.

References

Alberti, R. and Emmons, M. (1995) *Your Perfect Right: A Guide to Assertive Behavior* (seventh edition.) San Luis Obispo, California: Impact Publishers, (original, 1970).

Alberti, R. and Emmons, M. (1975) *Stand Up, Speak Out, Talk Back!* New York: Pocket Books.

Assagioli, R. (1971) *Psychosynthesis.* New York: Viking Press.

Astin, J. (1997). "Stress Reduction Through Mindfulness Meditation: Effects on Psychological Symptomatology, Sense of Control, and Spiritual Experience." *Psychotherapy and Psychosomatics,* 66:97-106.

Atkinson, B. (1950) *The Writings of Ralph Waldo Emerson.* New York: Random House.

Bernhard J. and Kabat-Zin J. (1988) Effectiveness of relaxation and visualization techniques as an adjunct to phototherapy and photochemotherapy of psoriasis. *Journal of the American Academy of Dermatology,* 19, 572-573.

Bohm, D. and Weber, R. (1982) The physicist and the mystic-Is a dialogue between them possible? In Wilber, K. (Ed.) (1982) , *In The Holographic Paradigm.* Boston: Shambhala.

Boswell, P. and Murray, E. (1979) Effects of meditation on psychological measures of anxiety. *Journal of Consulting and Clinical Psychology,* 47, 606-607.

Brunton, P. (1975) *The Quest of the Overself.* New York: Samuel Weiser, (original, 1937).

Brunton, P. (1970) *The Wisdom of the Overself.* New York: Samuel Weiser, (original, 1943).

Cassidy, C. M. (1994) Unraveling the ball of string: reality, paradigms, and the study of alternative medicine. *Advances: The Journal of Mind-Body Health.,* 10 (1), 5-31.

Chodorow, J. (Ed.) (1997) *Jung On Active Imagination.* Princeton, N.J.: Princeton University Press.

Corey, Gerald (1991) *Theory and Practice of Counseling and Psychotherapy.* Pacific Grove, Ca.: Brooks/ Cole.

Daumal, Rene (1952) *Mount Analogue.* New York: Penguin Books.

Embler, W.(1974) The metaphors of mysticism. *ETC: A Review of General Semantics,* 31, 3, 272-287.

Emmons, Michael L. (1978) *The Inner Source: A Guide to Meditative Therapy.* San Luis Obispo, Ca.: Impact Publishers.

Ferguson, M. (Ed.) (1982) A new perspective on reality. In Wilber, K. (Ed.), *The Holographic Paradigm.* Boston: Shambhala.

Frankl, V. (1913) *Affektstoerungen*. Berlin: Springer.
Frankl, V. (1969) *The Will to Meaning*. New York: The New American Library, Inc.
Frankl, V. (1960) *The Doctor and the Soul: From Psychotherapy to Logotherapy* (second edition). New York: Alfred A. Knopf.
Frederking, W. (1949) Deep relaxation with free ideation. *Psyche*, 2, 211.
Frederking, W. (1955) Intoxicant drugs (Mescaline and Lysergic Acid Diethylamide) in psychotherapy. *Journal of Nervous and Mental Disorders*, 121, No. 3, 262-266.
Frost, W.P. (1997) Is Evolution a Machine? *Advances, The Journal of Mind-Body Health*, 13, 3, 63-64.
Gaskell, G. (1960) *Dictionary of All Scriptures and Myths*. New York: Julian Press.
Goleman, D. (1974) Meditation as methatherapy, in White, J. (ed.), *What is Meditation?* New York: Anchor Books, 181-198.
Goleman, D. (1974) Meditation and psychic phenomena, in White J. (ed.), *What is Meditation?* New York: Anchor Books, 209-224.
Goleman, D. (1977) *The Varieties of Meditative Experience*. New York: E. P. Dutton.
Hannah, Barbara. (1981) *Encounters with the Soul: Active Imagination as Developed by C. G. Jung*. Santa Monica, California: Sigo Press.
Hannah, F., et al. (1965) Sex differences and relationships among neuroticism, extraversion, and expressed fears. *Perceptual and Motor Skills*, 20, 1214-1216.
Hellman, C., Budd, M., et al. (1990) A study of the effectiveness of two group behavioral medicine interventions for patients with psychosomantic complaints. *Journal of Behavioral Medicine*. Winter: 165-173.
Hesse, H. (1929) *Steppenwolf*. New York: Holt and Company.
Hesse, H. (1951) *Siddhartha*. New York: New Directions.
Huxley, A. (1972) Visionary Experience, in White, J. (ed.), *The Highest State of Consciousness*. New York: Anchor Books, 34-57.
Huxley, A. (1968) *Doors to Perception*. London: Chatto and Windus.
Huxley, A. (1961) Introduction to F.W.H. Meyers, in Smith, S. (ed.), *Human Personality and Its Survival of Bodily Death*. Hyde Park, New York: University Books, (original, 1903).
Jung, C.G. (1958) The psychological aspects of the Kore. *The Collected Works of C. G. Jung*. New York: Bollingen Foundation, XX, 9, 1, 190-193.
Jung, C. G. (1958) The concept of the collective unconscious. *The Collected Works of C.G. Jung*. New York: Bollingen Foundation, XX, 9, 1, 215.

Jung, C.G. (1958) The phenomenology of the spirit in fairytales. *The Collected Works of C.G. Jung*. New York: Bollingen Foundation, XX, 9, 1, 215.

Jung, C.G. (1958) A study in the process of individuation. *The Collected Works of C. G. Jung*. New York: Bollingen Foundation, XX, 9, 1, 352.

Jung, C.G. (1958) Two Essays on analytical psychology. *The Collected Works of C. G. Jung*. New York: Bollingen Founcation, XX, 7, 220.

Jung, C. G. (1958) Psychology and religion. *The Collected Works of C.G. Jung*. New York: Bollingen Foundation, XX, 11, 496.

Kabat-Zinn, J., et. al. (1992) Effectiveness of a meditation-based stress reduction program in the treatment of anxiety disorders. *American Journal of Psychiatry*, 149 (7), 936-943.

Kabat-Zinn, J. et. al. (1982) An outpatient program in behavioral medicine for chronic pain patients based on the practice of mindfulness meditation: theoretical considerations and preliminary results. *General Hospital Psychiatry*, 4, 33-42.

Kabat-Zinn, J. et. al. (1985) The clinical use of mindfulness meditation for the self-regulation of chronic pain. *Journal of Behavioral Medicine*, 8, 163-190.

Kabat-Zinn, J., et. al. (1986) Four-year follow-up of a meditation-based program for the self-regulation of chronic pain: treatment outcomes and compliance. *Clinical Journal of Pain*, 2, 159-173.

Kaplan, K., et. al. (1993) The impact of meditation based stress reduction program on fibromyalgia. *General Hospital Psychiatry*, 15, 284-289.

Kapleau, P. (1967) *The Three Pillars of Zen*. Boston: Beacon Press.

Kitselman, A. L. (1950) *E-Therapy*. La Jolla, California: Institute of Integration.

Kretschmer, W. (1972) Meditative techniques in psychotherapy, in Tart, C. (Ed.), *Altered States of Consciousness*. New York: Anchor Books, 224-233.

Kubler-Ross, E. (1969) *On Death and Dying*. New York: Macmillan.

Kubler-Ross, E. (1975) *Death, The Final State of Growth*. Englewood Cliffs, New Jersey: Prentice-Hall, Inc.

LeShan, L. (1974) *How to Meditate*. Boston: Little Brown and Company.

LeShan, L. (1997) The DSM 21: Introduction. *Advances: The Journal of Mind-Body Health*, 13, 67-69.

Levine, S. (1991) *Guided Meditation, Explorations, and Healings*. New York: Doubleday.

Luthe, W. (Ed.) (1969) *Autogenic Therapy*. New York: Grune and Stratton, Inc.

Luthe, W. (Ed.) (1969) *Autogenic Therapy, Volume 1: Autogenic methods,* by Schultz, J. and Luthe, W. New York: Grune and Stratton, Inc.

Luthe, W. (Ed.) (1969) *Autogenic Therapy, Volume II: Medical Applications,* by Schultz, J. and Luthe, W. New York: Grune and Stratton, Inc.

Luthe, W. (Ed.) (1969) *Autogenic Therapy, Volume III: Applications in Psychotherapy,* by Schultz, J. and Luthe, W. New York: Grune and Stratton, Inc.

Luthe, W. (Ed.) (1970) *Autogenic Therapy, Volume IV: Research and Theory,* by Luthe W. New York: Grune and Stratton, Inc.

Luthe, W. (Ed.) (1973) *Autogenic Therapy, Volume VI: Treatment With Autogenic Neutralization,* by Luthe, W. New York: Grune and Stratton, Inc.

McKay, M. (1989) *When Anger Hurts.* New York: Fine Communications.

Miller, E. (1994) *Letting Go of Stress.* Menlo Park, Ca.: Source Cassette Tapes.

Miller, J. (1993) The unveiling of traumatic memories and emotions through mindfulness and concentration meditation: clinical implications and three case reports. *The Journal of Transpersonal Psychology,* 25 (2), 169-180.

Moody, R. (1975) *Life After Life.* Atlanta: Mockingbird Books.

Moyers, B. (1993) *"Healing and the Mind."* Public Broadcasting Service.

Nugent, Frank A. (1994) *An Introduction to the Profession of Counseling.* Upper Saddle River, N.J.: Prentice-Hall.

Osis, K. (1960) *Deathbed Observations by Physicians and Nurses.* New York: Parapsychology Foundation.

Pascal, Eugene (1992) *Jung to Live By.* New York: Warner Books.

Rhine, J. and Pratt, J. (1957) *Parapsychology, Frontier Science of the Mind.* Springfield, Illinois: Charles C. Thomas.

Rogers, C. R. (1961) *On Becoming a Person.* Boston: Houghton Mifflin.

Rogers, C. R. (1973) Some new challenges. *The American Psychologist,* 28, 379-387.

Roth, B. (1997) Mindfulness-based stress reduction in the inner city. *Advances, The Journal of Mind-Body Health,* 13(4), 50-58.

Schultz, J.H. (1932) *Das Autogene Training.* Leipzig: G. Thieme Verlag.

Shapiro, F. (1995) *Eye Movement Desensitization and Reprocessing.* New York: The Guilford Press.

Smith, G. (Ed.) (1969) *Letters of Aldous Huxley.* London: Chatto and Windus.

Stanford, A. (translator) (1970) *The Bhagavad Gita*. New York: Seabury Press (Copyright Herber & Herber, Inc.)

Tart, C. (Ed.) (1990) *Altered States of Consciousness* (revised edition). New York: Harper and Row.

Tate, D. (1994). "Mindfulness Meditation Group Training: Effects on Medical and Psychological Symptoms and Positive Psychological Characteristics." Brigham Young University.

Teasdale, J. et. al. (1995) How does cognitive therapy prevent depressive relapse and why should attentional control (mindfulness) training help? *Behaviour Research and Therapy*, 33 (1), 25-39.

Weber, R. (1982) The physicist and the mystic- is a dialogue between them possible? A conversation with David Bohm, in Wilber, K. (Ed.) *The Holographic Paradigm*. Boston: Shambhala.

White, J. (Ed.) (1974) *What is Meditation?* New York: Anchor Books.

White, J. (Ed.) (1972) *The Highest State of Consciousness*. New York: Anchor Books.

White, J. (Ed.) (1974) *Frontiers of Consciousness*. New York: Avon Books.

Wilber, K. (Ed. (1982) *The Holographic Paradigm?* Boston: Shambhala.

Wilhelm, R. (translator) (1962) *The Secret of the Golden Flower*. New York: Harcourt Brace Jovanovich, Inc. (Harvest Book).

Wolpe, J. (1958) *Psychotherapy by Reciprocal Inhibition*. Stanford, California: Stanford University Press.

Wolpe, J. (1990) *The Practice of Behavior Therapy* (fourth edition). New York: Pergamon Press.

Index

Abreaction, 38, 42-44, 150, 151
Active imagination, 162-163
Active Imagination, 162
Advances, The Journal of Mind-Body Health, 22
Amenorrhea, 89
A New Perspective on Reality, 26
Assagioli, R., 162, 168
Assertiveness training, 100
Astin, J., 171
Atkinson, B., 176
Autogenic Abreaction Therapy, 162
Autogenic abreaction, 166-168
Autogenic Testing, 166
Autogenic Training, 34-35, 166

Behavioral therapy, 45
Behaviors, 130, 133, 142-144, 146
Bernhard, J., 171
Bhagavad Gita, 59, 165, 177
Bible, the, 59, 177
Bingeing, 142-143
Bohm, D., 24, 25, 26
Books of the Dead, 59
Boswell, P., 171
Brahman, 176
Brunton, P., 176
Buddha, 177

Cassidy, C., 22, 23, 24
Centennial, 107
Chandogya Upanished, 176
Child Protective Services, 141
Chodorow, J., 162-163
Christ, 47
Cinderella, 6
"Cleaning Cobwebs from My Mind" (The Case of Kerrie), 149
    evaluation, 157-159
    history, 150
    intervention and experiences, 150, 151-155
    presenting problem, 149
    results, 155-157
Client-centered therapy, 100
Client selection, 6, 33-35, 102-103

Cognitive behavioral events, 152-153
Cognitive behavioral theory, 51-52
Collage, 122-123
Community Health Center, 171
Concentrative meditation, 169
Concentrative technique, 116
Consciousness, 168-169
Consent for Meditative Therapy Treatment (form), 197
Control, 82-83
Core events, 131, 132, 136, 138
Core issues, 131, 136-137
Core met needs, 132, 139
Core strength, 132, 138-139
Counseling goals and techniques, 31
Counseling relationship, 31-32
Creative experiences, 57-58
    new, 72-74, 154
    parapsychological, 65-71, 154-155
    unusual light, 59, 60-65, 154
Creative Experiences in Meditative Therapy (figure), 58
Creative goal, 12-16

Daumal, R., 36, 57
Debriefing, 16-19, 110
Deep relaxation with free ideation, 163-164
Deep Relaxation with Free Ideation, 162
Devil, the, 122
Dianetic Foundation, 165
Diet, 150
Directing, 119-120
Directive statements, 104
Discarnate entities, 68-70
Discharging, 38, 39-40, 151
Drawing, 118, 122-123
Dream work, 118-119, 124
DSM IV, 22, 32

Eckhaart, M., 37
Educational and Industrial Testing Services (EDITS), 181
Embler, W., 177
Emerson, R., 176

Emmons, M., 185
E-therapy, 165-166
E-Therapy, 162, 165
Eva's core (case example), 136-139
Eva's Holistic Map (figure), 135
Events, negative, 129, 139-141
Events, positive, 132-133, 144-145
Existential theory, 50-51
Experiences, past, 131-132
Extended discharging, 38, 40-42, 152
Eye Movement Desensitization and
    Reprocessing (EMDR), 24, 99, 199,
    200
*Eye Movement Desensitization and
    Reprocessing,* 129, 162

Facilitating meditative therapy, 4-5, 99,
    114
    between session availability and,
        111-112
    client questions and, 103-104
    client selection and, 6, 33-35, 102-103
    debriefing and, 16-19, 110
    ending sessions and, 108-110
    follow-up and, 113
    homework and, 110-111, 121-122,
        124-126
    pre-session anxiety and, 113
    prompting and, 104-106
    recording and tracking process and,
        106-108
    session example, 9-19
    therapist and, 5, 33, 99-102
    See also Meditative therapy,
        enhancing
Fear Inventory Items (form), 181

Fears and resistance, 75, 83-85, 108
    losing control and, 82-83
    mental illness and, 77-79
    pain and discomfort, 79-82
    self-disclosure and, 76-77
Feelings, 130, 133, 141-142, 144, 145
Fergusen, M., 26, 27
Follow-up, 112-113

Follow-up of Counseling Form,
    185-187
Frankl, V., 168
Frederking, W., 162, 163, 164
Freud, S., 168
Fromm, E., 177
Frost, W., 25

Gestalt theory, 48-49, 153
God, 48, 65, 70, 96, 131, 165, 176, 177
Goleman, D., 169, 170, 171
Guided imagery, 116
Gurdjieff, G., 170

Hannah, F., 155
"Healing and the Mind," 171
Healing goal, 12, 13-16
Hellman, C., 171
Hesse, H., 3
Holistic Map (figure), 128
Holistic map, the, 127, 146-148
    current negative responses and,
        129-131
    current positive responses and,
        132-134
    Eva (case example), 134-148
    negative past experiences and,
        131-132
    positive past experiences and, 132
Holographic brain, 24-26
Holographic universe, 24-26
Holography, 3, 26-28
Homework, 110-111, 121-122, 124-12
Human nature, 30
Huxley, A., 59, 165, 168, 177
Hypnotherapy, 100

Inner-directed thought, 107-108
Inner source, 1-4, 26-28
Insight, 153
Integrative treatment, 38-39, 44-52
Interpreting, 120-126
*Introduction to the Profession of
    Counseling,* 30
Isaiah, 176

Jacobsen technique, 116
Jesus, 177
John 8, 177
Journaling, 124-125
Jung, C., 37, 64, 162, 163, 169, 177

Kabat-Zinn, J., 171, 172
Kaplan, K., 171
Kapleau, P., 176
Kitselman, A., 162, 165, 166
Kohlberg, L., 178

LeShan, L., 22
"Letting Go of Stress" (tape), 199
Levine, S., 200
Light experiences, unusual, 59, 60-65, 154
Like Water for Chocolate, 48
Lindbergh, 107
Luthe, W., 34, 35, 162, 166, 167
Lu-tsu, 37

McCartney, L., 137
Maladaptive behavior, 30-31
Managed care, 5
Manifestation of Various Types of Light Experience Occurring in a Group of 75 Counseling Clients (figure), 60
Maslow, A., 131, 162, 178
Meditation, 169-175
Meditative therapy, 1-2, 29-32
  benefits and, 35-36
  client characteristics and, 32-33
  considerations and contraindications, 6, 33-35
  enhancing, 115-126
  facilitating, 99-114
  introducing to clients and, 7-9, 103, 113-114
  outcomes and, 87-97
  questions about, 2-6, 193-195
  roots of, 161-178
  session example, 9-19
  ten important points and, 179
Meditative therapy, enhancing, 115
  directing, 119-120

interpreting, 120-126
  stimulating, 115-119
Meditative Therapy Follow-up Questionnaire, 157-159, 189-191
Mental illness, 77-79
Mescaline, 163
Metaphor, 45-46, 152
Miller, E., 199
Miller, J., 171, 172
Mindfulness meditation, 169-173
Moyers, B., 171
Murray, E., 171
Music, 116-117

New experiences, 72-74, 154
Nugent, F., 30

Osgood-Schlatter Disease, 42
Outcomes, meditative therapy, 87
  emotional, 88, 89-91, 93-94
  follow-up questionnaire and, 91-97
  physical, 87, 89, 95
  spiritual, 88, 91, 95-96

Outer-directed thought, 106-107
Out-of-body experiences (OOB's), 70-71

Pain and discomfort, 79-82
Paradigm and perspective, 21
  holographic universe and brain, 24-26
  inner source and, 26-28
  paradigm partnership and, 22-24
  psycho-spiritual synthesis and, 22
Parapsychological experiences, 65-71, 154-155
Parapsychology, The Frontier Science of the Mind, 65
Pascal, E., 163
Past lives experiences, 66-67
Physical sensations, 130, 133, 144, 146
Post-traumatic Stress Disorder (PTSD), 32, 89-91, 103
Pratt, J., 65
Precognition, 65-66

Pribram, K., 3, 24, 26, 27
Progressive muscle relaxation, 116
Prompting, 104-106
Psyche, 163
Psychoanalytic theory, 46, 47-48
Psychodynamic theory, 46-47
Psychosynthesis, 168
Psychotherapies, inner-oriented, 162
  active imagination, 162-163
  autogenic abreaction, 166-168
  deep relaxation with free ideation, 163-164
  E-therapy, 165-166
Putting away the disturbance (exercise), 202

Quixote, D., 107

Rational-emotive behavior therapy, 100
Recording and tracking process, 106-108
Reinforcement, 39, 54, 153
Relationships, 143
Resistance. See Fears and resistance
Responses, negative, 129-131
Responses, positive, 132-134, 144-146
Rhine, J., 65
Rogers, C., 24, 162
Roth, B., 171, 172
Rutgers University, 25

Safety and closure, creating, 199-202
Sand tray therapy, 117-118
Schultz, J., 166
Self-disclosure, 76-77
Sessions. See Facilitating meditative therapy
Shapiro, F., 129, 162, 199, 200
Siddartha, 3
Sleeping, 143-144
Smith, G., 165
Snickers Bars, 124
Spiritual responses, 130-131, 133-134, 144, 146
Spiritual traditions, 176-178
Stanford, A., 165, 177

Stanford University, 24
Supportive statements, 105
Symbols and images, 117
Systematic desensitization, 45

Tao, 23
Tart, C., 70
Tate, D., 171
Teasdale, J., 172
The Case of Kerrie (figures), 151, 155, 156
"The DSM 21: Introduction," 22
The light-stream exercise, 200-202
The process factor, 173-175
The purpose factor, 175
Thera, N., 170
Therapeutic experiences, 37
  abreaction and, 38, 42-44, 150, 151
  discharging and, 38, 39-40, 151
  extended discharging, 38, 40-42, 152
  healing goal and, 38-39
  integrative treatment and, 38-39, 44-52
  reinforcement and, 39, 54
  understanding and, 39, 52-53
Therapist preparation, 99-102
Theravadin Buddhism, 177
The safe space exercise, 199-200
The Secret of the Golden Flower, 59, 65, 177
The Stress Reduction and Relaxation Clinic, 171
The Therapeutic Healing Goal (chart), 38
The Three Pillars of Zen, 176
"The Unveiling of Traumatic Memories and Emotions Through Mindfulness and Concentration Meditation: Clinical Implications and Three Case Reports," 172
The Varieties of the Meditative Experience, 169
The Waltons, 111
Thoughts, 129-130, 133, 145
Traditional Acupuncture Institute, 22
Transcendental Meditation, 72, 161
Transcripts, 121-122

Understanding, 39, 52-53
University of California at Davis, 70
University of Dayton, 25
University of Massachusetts Medical
    Center, 171
Unmet needs, 131-132, 137-138

Verbal attacks, 143
"Visionary Experience" (lecture), 59
Visionary meditation, 162
Vissudhimaga, 169
Voice of America, 50

Weber, R., 25
*What Clients Want to Know About
    Meditative Therapy,* 19
What Clients Want to Know About
    Meditative Therapy (form), 193-195
White, J., 168, 176, 177
Wilber, K., 3, 25, 178
Wilhelm, R., 65, 177
Willoughby, R., 183
Willoughby Personality Schedule, 155,
    183-184
Wolpe, J., 155

Xanax, 52

Yoga, 176
Yosemite National Park, 153

Zen Buddhism, 176

The Practical Therapist Series®

Books in *The Practical Therapist Series* are designed to answer the troubling "what-do-I-do-now-and-how-do-I-do-it?" questions often confronted in the practice of psychotherapy. Written in plain language, technically innovative, theoretically integrative, filled with case examples, *The Practical Therapist Series* brings the wisdom and experience of expert mentors to the desk of every therapist.

Integrative Brief Therapy
Cognitive, Psychodynamic, Humanistic & Neurobehavioral Approaches
John Preston, Psy.D.
Hardcover: $27.95   272pp   ISBN: 1-886230-09-9
This thorough discussion of the factors that contribute to effectiveness in therapy carefully integrates proven elements of therapeutic efficacy from diverse theoretical viewpoints.

Rational Emotive Behavior Therapy
A Therapist's Guide
Albert Ellis, Ph.D., and Catharine MacLaren, M.S.W., CEAP
Hardcover: $22.95   176pp   ISBN: 1-886230-12-9
Up-to-date guidebook by the innovator of Rational Emotive Behavior Therapy. Includes thorough description of REBT theory and procedures, case examples, exercises.

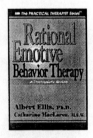

Creative Therapy with Children and Adolescents
Angela Hobday, M.Sc. and Kate Ollier, M. Psych.
Hardcover: $21.95   192pp   ISBN: 1-886230-19-6
Over 100 activities for therapeutic work with children, adolescents, and families. Simple ideas, fun games, fresh innovations to use as tools to supplement a variety of therapeutic interventions.

Metaphor in Psychotherapy
Clinical Applications of Stories and Allegories
Henry T. Close, Th.M.
Hardcover: $34.95   320pp   ISBN: 1-886230-10-2
Creative collection of stories and allegories, and how to use them as teaching tools in psychotherapy, by a highly respected Ericksonian psychotherapist.

Please see the following page for more books.

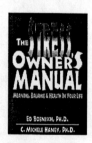